Praise for *The Hope*

"Every age has its teachers, who keep the eternal truths alive for all of us. In the case of Andrew Harvey, the light he sheds is like a meteor burst across the inner sky."

— **Marianne Williamson**, author
of *The Age of Miracles* and *Return to Love*

"If God created a new curriculum for the human race—one that might ensure our continued place on this planet—I think he would make **The Hope** *required reading. Andrew Harvey's wise and joyous prose brings home the necessary union of spiritual practice and radical action. But it does much more than that. It makes us want to roll up our sleeves and get to work. It seduces us to create change from the inside out, or as Gandhi said, to be the peace we long to see in the world. Prophets throughout the ages have said what Andrew Harvey is saying, but never in language as useful for our times. He joins the ranks of the great wise ones—the sages and the radicals—in his dream for a world of peace."*

— **Elizabeth Lesser**, co-founder, Omega Institute and
author of *Broken Open: How Difficult Times Can Help Us Grow*

"Andrew's work is a guidebook to a new world, much needed because it represents the hidden truth within the nature of great transformation; a new path of harmony always emerges out of the chaos of the present moment . . . **The Hope** *is destined to transform the lives of hundreds of thousands, if not millions, of people not only because of its profound message but also because we need his work more than we realize."*

— **Caroline Myss**, author of *Sacred Contracts* and *Defy Gravity*

"As an activist working with homeless people, I attempt to fuse together my deepest spiritual practice with action in the world, I've been waiting for a book that I could give to all my activist friends to help them meld inner peace and passion with wise and steady outer action. Andrew Harvey's **The Hope** is the book I have been waiting for. I urge all spiritual seekers concerned with the state of the world, and all the activists hungry for the new level of determination, peace, and energy, to read it and work with it."

— **Adam Bucko,** founder of the Reciprocity Foundation

"This book takes one on a great journey through profound experiences of many, including the author Andrew Harvey. It engages each one of us in the most important inquiry for today's world: who am I in the emerging narrative, in creating new patterns for a world that works or everyone? It is about the compassion of our sacred space and the courage to create alternatives where needed."

— **Dr. Monica Sharma,** director of Leadership and Capacity Development, United Nations-OHRLLS

"Andrew Harvey is one of the most important teachers of our times for his extraordinary capacity to marry the deep mystical teachings of our essential unity with awakened action. Sacred Activism is the yoga of the now; it inspires and guides our way into the challenge of Rebirth and great awakening. I will give and recommend **The Hope** to all!"

— **Shiva Rea,** yogini, catalyst of the Global Mala Project and Dance for Life: Moving Activism to Plant 1,080,000 Trees with Trees for the Future.

"True spirituality is love in action. **The Hope** will inspire you to grow into the most loving person you can be. Andrew Harvey calls you to make love the real work of your life. He wants you to love as if the future of the planet depended on it."

— **Robert Holden, Ph.D.,** author of Be Happy and Happiness NOW!

THE
HOPE

ALSO BY ANDREW HARVEY

THE DIRECT PATH

SON OF MAN

THE WAY OF PASSION

THE RETURN OF THE MOTHER

A JOURNEY IN LADAKH

SUN AT MIDNIGHT

THE ESSENTIAL MYSTICS

TEACHINGS OF RUMI

Please visit Hay House USA: **www.hayhouse.com**®
Hay House Australia: **www.hayhouse.com.au**
Hay House UK: **www.hayhouse.co.uk**
Hay House South Africa: **www.hayhouse.co.za**
Hay House India: **www.hayhouse.co.in**

THE
HOPE

A Guide to Sacred Activism

ANDREW HARVEY

HAY HOUSE, INC.
Carlsbad, California • New York City
London • Sydney • Johannesburg
Vancouver • Hong Kong • New Delhi

Published and distributed in the United States by: Hay House, Inc.: www.hayhouse.
com • *Published and distributed in Australia by:* Hay House Australia Pty. Ltd.:
www.hayhouse.com.au • *Published and distributed in the United Kingdom by:*
Hay House UK, Ltd.: www.hayhouse.co.uk • *Published and distributed in the
Republic of South Africa by:* Hay House SA (Pty), Ltd.: www.hayhouse.co.za •
Distributed in Canada by: Raincoast: www.raincoast.com • *Published in India
by:* Hay House Publishers India: www.hayhouse.co.in

Design: Tricia Breidenthal

Library of Congress Cataloging-in-Publication Data

Harvey, Andrew.
The hope : a guide to sacred activism / Andrew Harvey.
  p. cm.
Includes bibliographical references.
ISBN 978-1-4019-2003-6 (trade pbk. : alk. paper) 1. Religion and
    social problems. 2. Spiritual life. I. Title.
BL65.S64H37 2009

201'.7--dc22   2009018286

ISBN: 978-1-4019-2003-6

12 11 10 09   4 3 2 1
1st edition, September 2009

Printed in the United States of America

To

Jill Angelo
April Barrett
Diane Berke
Karuna Erickson
My mother, Kathleen Elizabeth Harvey
Sheryl Leach
Caroline Myss
Shiva Rea
Gabrielle Roth
Gloria Vanderbilt
Marianne Williamson
in whom I see and honor the Divine Feminine

To

Neil Di Lauro
Howard Rosenberg
Nathan Schwartz-Salant
Tony Zito
in whom I see and honor the Divine Masculine

Hope, like the gleaming taper's light,
Adorns and cheers our way;
And still, as darker grows the night,
Emits a brighter ray.

— OLIVER GOLDSMITH

CONTENTS

FOREWORD

When Andrew told me that he decided upon the title *The Hope*, I secretly breathed a sigh of relief. I felt that if he could have hope after years of acquiring research on topics such as the eco-crisis and the ever-present threat of nuclear terrorism, then there truly there was hope for all of us. Our present cycle of change has come with challenges so great that we are incapable of calculating all of them, much less comprehending the interconnected web of catastrophes these challenges portend. How can we comprehend or even imagine what tomorrow will bring? And I do mean tomorrow, as in "the next day." Already we have seen the monetary system collapse in a matter of days, something no one believed possible. But as we are learning, nothing is the same as it was even as recently as last year. We are, all of us, now headed into a very different world. Andrew's work is a guidebook to this new world, much needed because it represents a mystical truth hidden within the nature of great transformation: a new path of harmony always emerges out of the chaos of the present moment. Life will reorganize itself, renew itself, and find pathways of survival more suitable for the next generation.

And just as nature has deeply rooted impulses that direct it to map its route through the crisis of global transformation, so also does human nature. We are sensing this path of our own transformation in various ways, one of which is that many people are feeling a need to become active agents of change, which Andrew describes as a call to Sacred Activism. Having had the privilege of listening to Andrew lecture on the subject of Sacred Activism for five years, I have witnessed the impact the concept of action guided by sacred consciousness has on individuals, which in turn, have a transformational effect on all life. Andrew is quick to point out that action performed in concert with the sacred can take any form—from volunteering in shelters to investing in eco-projects to devoting twenty minutes a day to praying for people in crises. Andrew believes, as do I, that the time has come for you to recognize your capacity to make a difference, however small or grand, and that every action when done with consciousness of the Sacred adds to the healing of the whole life system. This is a mystical truth whose time has come—each of us has the power to make a difference in the lives of others and in our environment.

Andrew's work is destined to transform the lives of hundreds of thousands if not millions of people—not only because of its profound message but also because we need his work even more than we realize. Through my own work, I've come to understand that aside from the obvious social, political, economic, and environmental challenges facing us, there are even more treacherous subtle forces at play. I consider them even more treacherous because we pay them no mind, yet they are reshaping us like Silly Putty. Specifically, I am aware of how change is increasingly rapid. We cannot calculate how fast business, money, nations, politics, ideas, and laws—essentially anything and everything—changes. We can't keep up anymore, not with our families, not with our friends, and certainly not with ourselves. And of all the things in life we fear most, change is at the top of the list. So here we are, living in a world in which we are essentially out of control at light speed. Yet, no one is addressing this fact, much less the emotional, psychic, mental, or physical consequences of this crisis.

Additionally, every change is now global in magnitude. There is hardly such a thing as a "local" change. The Internet and the television have brought the changes of all nations into view within seconds and not only into view, but into your bank account, into your stock holdings, into your insurance policies, and into your job security. A shift in the market in Japan or China could result in the loss of your job in the morning. The world you go to sleep in is not the world you wake up in, so quickly move all forces these days.

And finally, all change is now profound. By profound, I mean that it has significance well beyond what we are able to grasp, much less do anything about as individuals *at the ordinary level of response.* We are now on continual overload with data and news and information that affects not only our exterior lives but also our emotional, psychological, and mental well-being. Rarely do we pause to consider this. I frequently hear people tell me that they avoid the news because it's all negative, but is avoidance really a mature response? If so, then who should respond to those assaulting the environment? And to those committing war crimes? And to those violating our Constitution? These crimes happened and will continue to happen precisely because people do not want to look at the shadow of the society we live in, much less the shadow of the global community.

But even without consciously listening to the news or reading a newspaper, the impact of these events seeps into your psyche and nervous system. You are now an electromagnetic human being, more energy than matter in your way of interacting with the communications systems of life. You want to be in touch with everything and everyone in a second. Don't imagine for a moment that the psychic free radicals generated by the collective unconscious are not penetrating into your individual psychic field, because they are. As I said, all change these days is profound and none of us can avoid that energy in the air we collectively breathe. And all of us get our fair share of psychic free radicals, I assure you.

It's time we realize that we have crossed the energy Rubicon. This new world of ours needs to be seen and understood and interacted with as an energetic system of power. We are living at a pivotal time in history because we are witnessing the decline of the age of matter and the rise of the age of energy, or the solar age. We are the midwives of this new birth, and already we are hooked on the solar, or energy, technology of this age in its physical expression, the Internet, cell phones, and computers.

But nothing technological can compare with the extraordinary beauty and power of the awakened human soul. The person that commits his or her creative energy toward being of service to humanity, knowing that every action now moves the world at a rapid speed and makes a profound difference, has set a course for personal and global illumination.

I believe that many people are now being called to be of service as Sacred Activists; that is, to bring the consciousness of the Sacred into all they do as agents of profound change. Such a commitment opens a shaft of grace that inspires a person to make a difference, whether privately or professionally. I also believe that we are never in a position to measure or judge the impact of our actions. It is not for us to know who or how many or in what way our actions will make a difference. If you need to know that, then as the great saint Teresa of Ávila would often say to her nuns, "You are not ready for the task. Go back in the kitchen and peel potatoes." To truly be of service, you must never judge what life asks you to do. Rather, see the Sacred in all things and in the smallest detail of your life. That, too, is an act of profound activism.

Andrew's vision of Sacred Activism has already given rise to an Institute, and I have no doubt his work and Institute will expand into many global Institutes of Sacred Activism. If, in reading this book, you are inspired to devote even ten minutes a day to another person, to give generously of yourself to another, then consider yourself well on your way.

Caroline Myss
Oak Park, Illinois

INTRODUCTION

A plump Indian businessman, dripping with gold and diamonds, came one day to visit Mother Teresa, fell at her feet, and proclaimed, "Oh my God, you are the holiest of the Holy! You are the super-holy one! You have given up everything! I cannot even give up one samosa for breakfast! Not one single chapati for lunch can I give up!"

Mother Teresa started to laugh so hard her attendant nuns grew scared (she was in her middle 80s and frail from two recent heart attacks). Eventually, she stopped laughing and, wiping her eyes with one hand, she leaned forward to help her adorer to his knees.

She said to him quietly, "So you say I have given up everything?" The businessman nodded enthusiastically. Mother Teresa smiled. "Oh, my dear man," she said, "you are so wrong. It isn't I who have given up everything; it is you. You have given up the supreme sacred joy of life, the source of all lasting happiness, the joy of giving your life away to other beings, to serve the Divine in them with compassion. It is you who are the great renunciate!" To the Indian businessman's total bewilderment, Mother Teresa got down on her knees and bowed to him. Flinging up his hands, he ran out of the room.

The tremendous and simple secret that Mother Teresa was trying to communicate to the businessman is the message at the core of all the world's spiritual revelations—that lasting happiness springs only from true love of the Divine, the world, and others, a true love that expresses itself tirelessly in wise and compassionate action. As the great Buddhist mystic Shantideva made clear:

All the joy the world contains
Has come through wishing happiness for others;
All the misery the world contains
Has come through wanting pleasure for oneself.

The other side of this tremendous secret—also proclaimed by the world's spiritual traditions—is that this true love of the Divine and others, when expressed in wise, compassionate action, can lead not only to lasting inner joy but also to profound transformation of outer reality. As Robert Kennedy said in 1966 so eloquently and accurately: "Each time a person stands up for an ideal, or acts to improve the lot of others, or strikes out against injustice, he or she sends forth a tiny ripple of hope. And crossing each other from a million different centers of energy and daring, those ripples build a current that can sweep down the mightiest walls of oppression and resistance."

When the inner joy Mother Teresa spoke of, the joy of compassionate service, is married to a practical and pragmatic drive to transform all existing economic, social, and political institutions, a radical and potentially all-transforming holy force is born. This radical holy force I call Sacred Activism.

A Sacred Activist is someone who is starting to experience the inner joy and outer effectiveness of this force, who knows that the profound crisis the world is in is challenging everyone to act from our deepest compassion and wisdom, and who is committed to being, in the face of growing chaos, suffering, and violence, what Robert Kennedy called "a tiny ripple of hope" and a "center of energy and daring."

Millions of people all over the world are now waking up to the need to become Sacred Activists. The collapse of the world's financial markets, the growing universal understanding that the environment is in serious danger and that a wholly new energy policy is urgently needed, and the menace of nuclear war in the Middle East and between India and Pakistan have started to change everything. The election of Barack Obama as the president of the United States, the focusing symbol of the free world, has opened up a new, sober, and urgent conversation about essential values, and the need for a radical transformation of our way of being is breaking out everywhere.

My hope is that the vision I am presenting here will inspire everyone who reads this book to become a Sacred Activist and so participate not only in the "preservation" of humanity, but in what I—and many other mystics of all traditions—believe to be the humbling and amazing transfiguration it is destined for. What we are being asked to do is not to "fix" the existing system but to radically transform it so we no longer, by our choices, threaten our lives and the lives of millions of species. And we can only do this by radically transforming ourselves.

What I pray that the vision of Sacred Activism will give you is the vision and the hope that will enable you to go through danger and difficulty with a tender heart, a peaceful mind, an increasingly supple and loving body, and a passionate, restless hunger to do all you can to preserve human and animal life on earth. I hope it will inspire you to help bring forth a new humanity and new world.

The secret of coming to live this great joy and hope in our time and to know its divine transformative power is given, I believe, in the following ancient Hindu story:

A beggar had been begging for days in a small dusty town without much success. Then, suddenly, he saw in the distance the golden chariot of the King appear. He started to dance for joy because his hopes rose high and he believed all dark days would soon be over. The King would throw him alms and wealth would gleam all around him in the dust. The King, however, confounded all his expectations by stopping the chariot and asking him what seemed to him like an outrageous question: "What have *you* got to give to *me?*" The beggar thought it was some kind of incomprehensible, even mad, joke. What could he, a beggar, have to give to the One who had everything? Gingerly, with some reluctance, and a little stunned, the beggar took one tiny little grain of corn out of the small bag he always carried with him to munch on. When at day's end he came to empty the bag out on the floor of his hut, he found, to his great surprise, that one of the grains of corn had turned to gold. And the beggar wept and wished that he had had the heart and passion and wisdom to give the King everything.

The reason this story is so suited to our time is that it points to *how* the Divine will rescue us from ourselves. It will not rescue us by some dramatic "intervention"; that is childish fantasy. The Divine will not intervene in such a way because it has something far more wonderful to give us than what we think we want and need. What it is offering us is our truest and most transformed selves, our hearts and minds and bodies increasingly "turned to gold" through the joy of putting Love into action—the joy of giving everything away for Love in Love as a part of Love.

What is being prepared for us is a life infinitely richer and more exciting than the hectic, anxious, gizmo-dominated, dissociated, dulled life so many of us are living now with such destructive consequences. The crisis that is exploding everywhere will clear away our addictions and the stony separation we have cultivated in the guise of wisdom to baptize us in a new passion of compassion and in inspired creativity.

In times of prosperity, you can sleep your whole life through, imagining that God's responsibility is just to keep the party going with all possible kinds of party favors. Faced with real danger, however, such smugness, entitlement, and complacency have no hope of surviving. You come to the end of the fantasy that the Divine is there to give *you* what *you* want. Slowly, painfully, but with more and more authentic hope and authentic joy, you start to suspect that we are here not to bask in God's love, but— willingly, freely, and with answering love—to give all we have to Love's work of transformation so Love can transform all we have, all we are, to gold.

It is in surrendering to this greatest of all laws of alchemy that we discover and *become* the real gold, the real power, the real hope. The terrible crisis we have manifested out of the addictions of our false self, if we learn its lessons, will lead us out of darkness into Light, out of the darkness of a relentless egoism that fuels destruction into a Light in which all we are and all we do can turn increasingly to the Divine. Just to imagine such a possible outcome of our difficulty is to be thrilled by hope; to start working for it with all you have and all you are is to start to live in a joy and peace that

Introduction

are *in* this world but not *of* it. There is no holier or more exciting life than this. And it is now being held out to anyone who dares to believe, hope, and work for it.

Teilhard de Chardin, the great Catholic mystic, wrote: "The day will come when, after harnessing space, the winds, the tides, gravitation, we shall harness for God the energies of love. And, on that day, for the second time in the history of the world, man will have discovered fire."

My deepest prayer for the vision of Sacred Activism is that it will inspire you to harness the energies of love, both in yourself and with others, and to discover, with wonder and hope, the joy and power of the "fire" that Teilhard describes—that fiery passion of compassion that, when allied with grounded wise action, will help us change everything.

The Hope is constructed as a journey into the power, truth, and radical holy force of Sacred Activism that unfolds in three stages or parts.

In Part I, I invite you into the heart of the hope for a new world through ten suggestions for immediate action, a set of initiatory and illuminating personal memories and stories, and an account of the expanding urgency of my vision of Sacred Activism. This hope, as you will see, is rooted in three main truths: the realization that all human beings have Divine Consciousness as their birthright and possess a greater capacity for courage, generosity, and selfless service than they may believe; the growing awareness that our current crisis is most creatively understood as a crisis of birth, the birth of a Divine Humanity out of the "death" of its narcissistic fantasies, beliefs, and agendas; and the understanding that the force of Sacred Activism is the lucid, passionate, and divinely blessed midwife of this birth.

In Part I, I present my vision of Sacred Activism in an anecdotal way, largely rooted in my own life journey. In Part II, I try to make as clear and objective as possible the nature of the illumined hope we need to infuse and inspire us if we are to continue as Sacred Activists with joy and courage. This is followed by a description of the "death" our world is undergoing and the "birth" this crisis is awakening; I show how a perfect storm of dangers is menacing the human race and a large part of nature with destruction and, at the same time, compelling and invoking from us unprecedented levels of creativity and enlightened passion for transformation in every realm. I end Part II with a concrete and pragmatic vision of the five kinds of service we will need to fuse in the core of our lives to become empowered Sacred Activists and, thus, humble and effective midwives of the "birth" starting to take place everywhere.

In Part III of *The Hope,* I present what I believe to be the Seven Laws of Sacred Activism—the seven mystical laws that both define what Sacred Activism is and shape its mysterious power and success in the world. On my own journey into the vision and practice of Sacred Activism, I have discovered, often through my mistakes and suffering, how essential it is to follow the lucid, grounded, and wise guidance of the world's spiritual traditions as to how we can act from sacred consciousness. Only action informed by this wisdom can become the channel for the power of Divine Grace.

The Seven Laws I present in Part III are those laws I myself—and other Sacred Activists through history—have experienced as the most inspiring, empowering, and practical. They are rigorous, but I have found that once you accept and practice their truth, you become grateful to know them, because understanding them and following them gives peace, energy, wisdom, and a sense of profound protection. What I pray to be able to convey is my growing understanding that, if these laws are followed precisely and humbly, their observance leads to nothing less than the emergence of Divine Consciousness in heart, mind, soul, and body and to the birth, both in each of us and in society as a whole, of new levels of divine blessing, compassion, harmony, and justice.

The Hope: A Guide to Sacred Activism ends with a description of the vision and practice of the Networks of Grace I am establishing, which will be a powerful, fresh way of organizing Sacred Activists in their local communities. I will also outline the Global Curriculum I am putting together and plan to disseminate in various ways using mass media, which will offer, to anyone who wants it, a precise, pragmatic summary of the vision and practices necessary to become effective Sacred Activists.

My prayer for this book is that in it you will find both the richest, most inspiring vision I can provide of what Sacred Activism is and the tools you will need to immediately start becoming a Sacred Activist.

May hope guide you, wisdom illumine you, and Divine Love fill you with its passion of compassion! Any merits this book may have I dedicate to all of you who are now reading this and to all sentient beings. As Pythagoras said: "Take courage, for human nature is divine."

PART I

"The world stands upon three things:
Upon Truth.
Upon Peace.
Upon Justice.
'Speak truth to the other, establish peace
and render honest judgment in your gates.'
(Zech 8:16)"

— Rabban Ben Gamliel

CHAPTER 1

TEN THINGS YOU CAN DO RIGHT NOW

Let me offer you ten things you can do right now, or within the next 24 hours, to start to align yourself with the power and hope of Sacred Activism. The first six will invite you into deep, nourishing connection with your spirit; the last four will help you express the compassion and joy this connection awakens in you in action.

1. Write down one thing that has made you feel grateful to be alive today. It could be something as simple as the taste of the bagel you had for breakfast or the sight of squirrels gamboling in the snow in the park. Get a small notebook and make the commitment to continue writing down one thing every day that lights you up with joy. At the end of the month, sit down and read the list out loud, slowly, to yourself. You will discover that it reminds you how blessed you are just by being alive in a world full of ordinary wonders. You will discover, too, that it awakens in you a passion for life and a hunger to protect and preserve it.

2. Now write down, without thinking too much or editing yourself—just "off the top of your heart"—ten things you would

say are sacred to you. Today my list is: friendship; all you who are reading this; justice; cats; the first roses of summer; all religions; wise elders everywhere who share their wisdom tenderly and tactfully; India; my brave and wild mother; and the voice of Maria Callas, which has guided me for 40 years into my own truest passion. What is your list? You will find that just by writing it down you will start to be inspired by your deepest values, beliefs, and sources of emboldening joy.

3. Think of someone who has hurt you or betrayed you and make a commitment to work on forgiving him or her. Imagine this person in front of you, surrounded by light, happy and well. Pray for this person to realize his or her life's purpose. Just doing this once with humble sincerity will unveil your innate strength of compassion. You will taste its truth and freedom and the desire that is born from it to see all beings happy.

4. Read a short text from any of the world's spiritual traditions that inspires you with the love-wisdom of the prophets and mystics who know God directly. The one I use daily is from Rumi:

O Love, O pure deep Love, be here, be now
Be all; worlds dissolve in your endless stainless radiance
Frail living leaves burn with you brighter than cold stars
Make me your servant, your breath, your core.

5. When the text you have chosen starts to light up your spirit, pray a short prayer that aligns you with the pure deep love that is longing to use you as its instrument in the world. Here are four, from different traditions, that I use at odd moments throughout my day:

Lord, let me live to be truly useful.

Beloved, make me strong enough to do Your will.

Divine Mother, fill me with your passion of compassion so I can do Your work tirelessly.

For as long as space exists and sentient beings remain, may I too remain to dispel the misery of the world.

If none of these prayers inspire you or reflect your beliefs, make up your own and say it ten times, with passion, in the core of your heart.

6. Make a real commitment to spiritual practice. If you do not yet have a practice, start now with a simple meditation. Just sit with your back straight and watch your thoughts for three minutes. Allow your mind, however briefly, to fall silent. In that silence is your greatest treasure, one that will unfold its gold in you if you commit to 20 minutes of simple sitting in the morning and again in the evening before you go to bed. Don't believe me; try it. If you find sitting and watching your thoughts boring, try this visualization that I received from a great Tibetan master who told me it could be used anytime, anywhere: "Imagine that love and compassionate action have transformed you into a large, brilliant diamond that radiates diamond-white light. Send that light to all the four directions, praying, with whatever words you choose, that all sentient beings everywhere be happy, well, and protected."

Over time, this meditation will awaken you to your own deepest sacred desire to see all beings living in harmony and true realization, and to your deepest sacred courage to express this desire in action. When you have begun to experience the beauty of this practice, start doing it at different times in your day—anytime, anywhere. You will be amazed at its power to bring you home to your most compassionate self.

7. Strengthened by prayer, practice, and inspiration, turn now to your life and the people in it. Everyone, especially in a time like ours, has friends who are grieving, or ill, or looking for a job, or in real financial difficulty. Commit now to ringing one of them

up and asking him or her what you could do to make the burden easier. Do this soon and be happy that you can.

8. Make a commitment to skip one meal in the coming 24 hours and send a check for the money you would have spent on it to a reputable organization dealing with world hunger. I strongly recommend Buddhist Global Relief (BGR). BGR focuses on providing food aid to the hungry of the third world and supporting projects designed to develop better long-term methods of food production and management; it is run economically and by devoted people. Visit their Website (www.buddhistglobalrelief.org) for further details. Any contribution, even as little as five dollars, will help far more than you can imagine. Never forget that almost two billion people live on less than a dollar a day.

9. The global crisis we are now facing is plunging people everywhere into distress. There are people around you who are suffering. Make a commitment to find out who they are and what they need, and invite six of your friends to make a commitment with you to begin supplying it. In acting like this, you will be helping to activate the heart of your community. In my experience, more people than you may imagine are longing to be of help; take the first step now yourself and be surprised and heartened.

10. Make a commitment today, even if you are having financial difficulties, to tithe between five and ten percent of what you earn to a cause of your choice. I recommend choosing one particular cause that deeply moves you. Over time, tithing will give you a great and healing sense of being useful and the cause you are helping will become more and more precious and personal to you so that you will want, naturally and simply, to do more. I have tithed for several years now to the cause of keeping the white Siberian tigers alive; it gives me happiness to think that because of the little I can give, two or three of those magnificent and noble creatures might be able to live. Whatever cause really moves you, move to be of help now. Don't wait. There is great suffering all around us,

and it is likely to get worse. Responding now will empower you immediately.

And one last suggestion, because 11 is a sacred number—the number of the hexagram Tai in the I Ching, which means "peace" and, in the words of Richard Wilhelm's commentary, "denotes a time in nature when heaven seems to be on earth." Make a commitment to keep some small change in one of your pockets so you can always give something to one of the growing thousands of homeless in our streets. I learned this habit as a child from my grandmother in India, and over the years it has brought me into contact with some extraordinary people. One in particular I would like to celebrate here. Outside a temple in South India, there was a long line of desolate-looking beggars and among them a very old woman, dressed in a ragged and filthy sari, with no shoes. I gave her what I had on me, about a dollar. I watched in amazement as she walked unsteadily over to the nearest food stand, bought a handful of chapatis, broke them carefully in two, and shared them with a dog as emaciated as she was.

If we all knew what that penniless old beggar knew, the hundreds of children who have died of starvation while you were reading this chapter would still be alive.

CHAPTER 2

INSPIRATIONS

I had the honor once of being at an intimate gathering in Paris with Nelson Mandela. He spoke to us, calmly and humbly, about the 27 years of imprisonment he had endured and of the lessons he had learned. At the end, none of us could say anything. Then someone asked him if he could sum up what he knew now, at this stage of his life (he was in his early 80s at the time). He thought for a long time and then began: "There is a force in the universe—call it God or spirituality or whatever you like—that wants the victory of truth and justice. This force will help you if you are steady, humble, brave, and patient. Never, ever give up, however bad things get." And then he smiled a smile that had the force of soft lightning.

In 1989 I was in Oslo to attend the celebrations for the awarding of the Nobel Peace Prize to His Holiness the Dalai Lama. I shall never forget the joy that radiated everywhere and shone in the faces of even the stodgiest-looking Norwegian officials when that holy, kind man walked up, smiling and waving and bowing, to receive the prize. For all the worldly pomp, everyone knew it was a sacred occasion, and many shed tears of gratitude for the life of the man before them. He has done more than anyone else I know to demonstrate the force of Sacred Activism in the middle of horror and tragedy.

The day before, I had interviewed His Holiness for *Elle* magazine. At the end of our hour together, spent in his small, bare hotel room, I stood up, plucked up my courage, and asked him, "What is the meaning of life?" His Holiness flung back his head and roared with laughter. Then he grew intensely concentrated and still. "The meaning of life," he said quietly, leaning forward to touch my forehead with his, "is to embody compassion. Anyone can discover this. When you discover this and live it, you discover your truest nature and share its joy."

In 2000, on a stormy gray day, I stood on the beach in Galilee where Jesus is said to have appeared to his disciples for the last time. It was a small, pebbly, utterly unremarkable beach, but something in its atmosphere brought me to my knees. Although I have a lover's quarrel with the churches erected in his name, Jesus has always been the greatest love of my heart. I loved him as a small boy, and I shall love him until the day I die; I pray always that my last thoughts will be of him.

It was on this beach that Jesus ate a meal of freshly caught fish with Peter and a group of other disciples. I had my small family Bible with me, and I turned to the last chapter of St. John's Gospel and read out these words quietly:

> So when they had dined, Jesus saith to Simon Peter, "Simon son of Jonas, lovest thou me more than these?" He saith unto him, "Yea, Lord; thou knowest that I love thee." He saith unto him, *"Feed my lambs"*
>
> He saith unto him again the second time, "Simon, son of Jonas, lovest thou me?" He saith unto him, "Yea, Lord, thou knowest that I love thee." He saith unto him, *"Feed my lambs"*
>
> He saith unto him the third time, "Simon, son of Jonas, lovest thou me?" Peter was grieved, because he said unto him the third time, "Lovest thou me?" And he said unto

him, "Lord, thou knowest all things, thou knowest that I love thee." Jesus saith unto him, *"Feed my sheep."*

I had known these words since my earliest childhood, but until that day I had never experienced their full force. That day I understood that when the love that moves the sun and stars starts to become real inside you, it compels you to act in whatever way you can to "feed my sheep." That is how you know that you are starting to become an authentic spiritual being.

When I lived in Paris in my 30s, I had a friend who was in her early 80s and lived in a studio with two blind dogs and a cat with three legs. In her youth she had acted in a series of bad films that made her rich and briefly famous. Until the age of 50, she told me, she "never had a serious thought in [her] head and lived an idiotic life." At 50, however, everything changed. Film parts started to dry up; she invested her money with a Moroccan financier who ran off to Marrakesh; her much-loved but much-neglected son was killed in a car accident; a lover used, humiliated, and betrayed her with one of her best friends. Alone and depressed, she sold her houses and dresses and bought a one-room studio in a remote, dangerous suburb of Paris. For a year she cut herself off from her old friends and lived on bread, cheese, and vegetables she scrounged from shopkeepers who remembered her as a minor queen of French cinema.

Her life did not change because she had a vision or met a master or suddenly fell in love with God. "I did not meet Jesus," she used to say tartly, "I met a dog." One afternoon she was wandering stoned, hungry, and desolate around her dingy neighborhood, wondering why she bothered to go on living at all, when quite suddenly, as if from nowhere, a small, knife-thin, clearly starving mutt with big floppy ears tottered toward her out of a doorway and fell at her feet. "I was so stoned and lost," she told me, "my first instinct was a kind of anger. How dare the dog do this to me? How dare I be reminded that there might be beings on the earth suffering even more than me? I wanted to kick it in the teeth." She did not kick the dog, however; she knelt down in the filthy street, took him up in her arms, took him home to her studio, nursed him back to health, and kept him with her until he died peacefully in his sleep ten years later, "the smelliest but without a doubt the most spoiled dog in Paris."

What she discovered on that afternoon went beyond even the joy of rescuing one helpless and abandoned creature. What she discovered was the cause she would devote herself to that saved her life and restored her hope: animal rights.

My friend couldn't stand Brigitte Bardot's bizarre neo-fascist politics, but she revered her for her vociferous, "magnificently annoying" tirades that tried to remind the French, as my friend said, "that animals are for more than just keeping meat fresh." She became a tireless rescuer of abandoned animals. She never made any real money again, but with the tiny amounts that came in from radio and TV appearances and a hilarious and scabrous memoir, she bought an old red-and-blue van and transported animals who had been found abandoned and abused to friendly homes.

I rang her one day and asked her, "Are you happy?" She paused and then said softly, "I'm happier than I've ever been. And not because I made those films all those years ago. I don't even know who that woman was, and I'm not sure I care. What an idiot she looks in all those period wigs. What makes me happy is that I know I have saved some lives—not for long, of course, since Mr. Death gets us all in his bag in the end, but perhaps for long enough for a few animals to know that not every human being is a self-centered"—and here she used a favorite French word, *crapaud,* which translates into (I'm being euphemistic) "arrogant bastard."

Two weeks later I was at her funeral. It was held in her squalid neighborhood, in a crumbling anonymous hall. No one from the film or theater world came, which would have amused her, although a few inaccurate obituaries peppered the more upmarket daily papers. Jacques Chirac, then mayor of Paris, sent a wreath of laughably bedraggled roses, which would also have amused her, because she once told me that of all living beings she despised him the most. Her friends read her favorite poems aloud, played her favorite Edith Piaf songs, and drank down rivers of red wine in her honor.

That was touching enough, but what made her funeral one of the most poignant and celebratory of any I have attended is that the music and poetry and laughter and half-drunk reminiscences were punctuated by one constant, wild, glorious sound— the sound of dozens of dogs of all kinds and sizes barking in chorus. About 80 people had traveled from all over France to honor my friend and her fight for animal rights, bringing with them the dogs she had once brought them in her battered van. The greatest eulogy she could ever receive was that yapping chorus of the dogs her fierce compassion had saved. There was a great deal of cleaning up of what we called "dog-ma" afterward, which would have amused her, too.

I tell you my friend's story not only because I loved and admired her but because I want to make certain that you know I respect—even revere—anyone who wants to help others, whatever his or her faith or lack of it. In fact, I have always felt a lot more at home with people who don't give a fig for any kind of conventional religion or even for "spirituality," but who do something practical to help others, than with so-called seekers who quote from the Dhammapada and the "Little Flowers of Saint Francis" with eyes raised to heaven and do nothing to help anyone. As for those who use a debased and narrow understanding of karma or of "divine order" to justify doing nothing in the face of the troubles of our time, I have to pray for grace so as not to want to hit them on the head with a saucepan. Give me an atheist activist over a smug and passive so-called seeker any day. I believe that all of us, whatever our faith or lack of it, are being challenged to act out of our deepest ethical concerns and conscience.

I also believe, however, that Sacred Activists are being invited to realize, in the core of their own lives, not only the joy and meaning that comes from being truly useful to others, but something even more transformative. They are being invited to experience for themselves how, when human beings turn consciously to the Divine in whatever form they know it and dedicate themselves humbly to a transformation that can make them instruments of Divine Love, they become individual, living fields of Divine Grace—empty vessels that can be filled with Divine Power in ways that seem wondrous, even miraculous, to others.

CHAPTER 3

TWO STORIES
OF SACRED
ACTIVISM

I have chosen the two central stories featured in this chapter because they speak vividly of the two sides of Sacred Activism—its power of Love that can transform even the most terrible circumstances and the most hardened human beings, and its power of Wisdom that may be able to transform even the natural environment itself.

Such a distinction between the two stories has an arbitrary element—the Love that is displayed so movingly in the first story arises from the inner wisdom of compassion, and the Wisdom that manifests its power in the second has its roots in a long practice of love for all beings. Yet I have found for myself that contemplating the potential reach and effectiveness of both approaches, both separately and together, can lead to startling revelations.

The two stories I want to offer did not take place in mystical or medieval times; they happened in the thick of today's crisis, in the very kinds of dangerous situations that threaten our future. The first is taken from the reports of the Truth and Reconciliation Commission in South Africa, a body established after the abolition of apartheid to bring its violence to light and give both victims and perpetrators a chance to be heard.

The Commission brought an elderly black woman face to face with the white man, Mr. Van de Broek, who had confessed to the savage torture and murder of her son and her husband a few years earlier. The old woman had been made to witness her husband's death. The last words her husband spoke were "Father, forgive them."

One of the members of the Commission turned to her and asked, "How do you believe justice should be done to this man who has inflicted such suffering on you and so brutally destroyed your family?"

The old woman replied, "I want three things. I want first to be taken to the place where my husband's body was burned so that I can gather up the dust and give his remains a decent burial." She stopped, collected herself, and then went on. "My husband and son were my only family. I want, secondly, therefore, for Mr. Van de Broek to become my son. I would like for him to come twice a month to the ghetto and spend a day with me so that I can pour out to him whatever love I have still remaining with me. And finally, I want a third thing. I would like Mr. Van de Broek to know that I offer him my forgiveness because Jesus Christ died to forgive. This was also the wish of my husband. And so, I would kindly ask someone to come to my side and lead me across the courtroom so that I can take Mr. Van de Broek in my arms, embrace him, and let him know that he is truly forgiven."

The assistants came to help the old black woman across the room. Mr. Van de Broek, overwhelmed by what he had just heard, fainted. And as he did, those in the courtroom—friends, family, neighbors, all victims of decades of oppression and injustice—began to sing "Amazing Grace."

The first time I read this sacred story in *Towards a Spirituality for Global Justice* by Elaine Prevallet, one detail leapt out and felled me with its truth: "Mr. Van de Broek, overwhelmed by what he had just heard, fainted." Nothing in his brutal and degraded past could have prepared Mr. Van de Broek for what the black woman gave him in return: not fury, not a call for his execution, but unconditional forgiveness and a reclaiming of him into the human family and into her own family. And the sacred power, flowing through her because of her humility and faith, did not merely move Mr. Van de Broek; it fell on him like invisible lightning from a dimension of pure love he might never have begun to suspect existed. In that moment, two extraordinary journeys, both terrible in different ways, intersected in an explosion of grace.

You might be deeply moved by this story but think that its relevance to the gritty reality of world affairs is marginal. This is a mistake. Anyone who has been involved with the Palestine-Israel and the India-Pakistan conflicts—the two most dangerous conflicts in our world—must know by now that a purely political solution, a shifting of boundaries or an exchange of money or power, has only a very small chance of success. In such extreme situations, only extreme solutions born from another dimension of truth and compassion have any real chance of being effective. There will be no end to the potential horror in the Middle East and in the India-Pakistan conflict in Kashmir until a great many people on both sides have made the amazing and humbling journey to unconditional forgiveness, not from a position of weakness or defeat, but from a mysterious inner experience of the nature of God as all-embracing Mercy. While dauntingly difficult, such a journey is by no means impossible; countless numbers of anonymous and so-called ordinary beings have made it throughout history and are making it now in Rwanda, Darfur, Cambodia, and the Congo, even amid storms of terror.

The embrace of unconditional forgiveness is essential to the success of all the major activist adventures in our world. There may be truth in the savage denunciation of corrupt corporations, politicians, and a media in bed with what Robert Kennedy called "systems of cold evil" that want to keep exploiting the earth. But this response has two main disadvantages in practical affairs: the excitement of projecting your own unacknowledged darkness onto others keeps you from seeing just how implicated you are. Advocating for any cause in this spirit virtually ensures your efforts will increase resistance rather than heal. Human beings will never be convinced to change their ways by other human beings who try to humiliate them. In nearly every case, such condemnation only reinforces the behavior it is trying to end. When people are accused of acts they know they are guilty of by others who have contempt for them, they almost always retreat even further into their self-destructive behavior. If they do change, it is from fear, or perhaps hypocrisy, but not from their own truth.

One of the main reasons the environmental movement has failed to win more people to its cause is because of the fierce moralism of many of its pronouncements and the attitude many environmental activists project that they and they alone are "right," while the rest of humanity is almost worthy of the extinction they are engineering. Of course it is hard to avoid feeling self-righteousness and disdain when speaking to people you believe are perpetuating outrageous abuses. Only radical "shadow work" (psychological work on your own largely unacknowledged dark aspects) and incessant prayer open the doors to the kind of humility in which you no longer view those opposed to what you believe as "other" but approach them with respect and compassion. The most effective negotiators in situations of extreme danger or conflict are always those whose experience of their own continuing inner conflicts makes them humble; they work to include others, even those who have continually indulged in acts of brutality and destruction.

It would be overly sentimental to imagine that negotiators who work in this spirit always succeed. What we can say, however, is that their path shows us the way to the only solutions that can succeed in the long run. These solutions are effective because they are rooted not only in a rational rearrangement of practical demands but also in a fundamental change of heart that can, in the right circumstances, cause a shift as profound as the one that felled Mr. Van de Broek.

Let me give you an example from my own experience that shows how I was inspired and changed by the story of the elderly black woman. Last year a man who had read my book on Rumi, *The Way of Passion*, wrote to me and told me that he was serving a 20-year jail sentence for torturing animals. He said he knew that the same horrifying impulses that had led him to such brutality still lived inside him, and he was writing to ask me for my help.

I can still remember my sorrow and horror at reading his letter. The torture of children and animals torments me so much that I know I have difficulty taking a balanced view of either subject. But I knew, too, that any disgust I allowed to linger in my heart toward this man would pervert any words of comfort or encouragement I could offer him. I would have no hope of helping him if I did not aim for the height of unconditional love that the woman in the story spoke from. If she could forgive the man who had murdered her own husband and son, who was I not to try and forgive this man?

I prayed for days to be given the strength to respond to him in a way untainted by self-righteousness or revulsion. I had to face three things: an animal torturer existed in me too, as it does in anyone who, however momentarily, enjoys power over the weak or helpless; the man who had done these terrible things had had terrible things done to him; and while the animals he had tortured and killed were dead, he was still alive and in need of understanding and compassion, all the more so now that he was beginning to see and feel the horror of his actions.

The combination of these three perspectives, meditated on for days, finally gave me the strength, peace, and inner balance to write to him sincerely and, I hope, without any trace of condemnation. I told him frankly how I had felt when I read his letter, and I told him of the journey his honesty had impelled me on. I thanked him for it because if I had not been forced to take it, I would still have been unconsciously separating myself from people who had done the things he had, imagining myself to be superior and incapable of such brutality.

He and I wrote to each other several more times, and with each new account of the cruelty and neglect he had undergone as a child and the various criminal institutions he had lived in most of his life, my compassion for him and admiration for his transformation grew. Would I have had the courage to believe I could change after doing what he had done? Would I have had the stamina to unlearn the kind of lacerating self-hatred he had had to endure? I am not sure. In his last letter to me he wrote: "Thank you above all for making me feel that I have given *you* something. You will never know what that has meant to me. It has meant everything. It has given me a hope that saves me again and again from drowning in despair."

Two weeks after receiving this letter, I had occasion to sit down with the head of one of the most environmentally destructive corporations in the world. Because I had studied the record of this corporation in certain South American countries, I knew much more than I wanted to about both the brutal dealings of the corporation and the CEO himself. I had no illusions, of course, that an hour spent with Andrew Harvey would effect a change of heart and result in an immediate worldwide shift in corporate energy policy. I did know, however, that this was a cynical man who had the lowest opinion of "whiny, self-righteous environmentalists" and an even lower one, if possible, of religious leaders whom he referred to contemptuously (he was British) "as a bunch of hypocritical and bone-headed wankers." He had consented to see me because he was intrigued by my Oxford professorial background and had heard one of my tapes and thought it "almost interesting," which for him, I gathered, was high praise.

In the days before we met, I found myself asking what the elderly black woman would do faced with a man like this, who in his own way had committed or abetted crimes perhaps even greater than those of the Afrikan torturer? The more I asked the question, the clearer the answer became. She would go in and sit opposite him and see him as he really was—not as a criminal, but as the lost and bewildered human being he must be to have enslaved himself to the religion of power. She would sit before him knowing that he was an aspect of her. She would sit before him and pray to be the empty channel of a love and mercy and intelligence far greater and wiser than her own, in the hope that she would know what to say and how to say it.

I prayed for days before the meeting to be worthy of the elderly black woman's example. As it happened, the heavens did not open, the CEO certainly did not faint, and no one sang "Amazing Grace." But because of the attitude I walked in with (and no doubt because of his genuine goodwill), two small, subtle miracles did take place that neither of us could have imagined. We liked each other; freed of the need to condemn him, I could appreciate his brilliance, his wit, his love of cricket and classical music, the genuine if sporadic charm that showed through his incessant need to dominate and manipulate. Because I did not attack or humiliate him, he was able to admit at the end of our conversation that it was "essential to start up a conversation about ethics in corporate activity." I have no idea if he will make good on his promise or whether what he said was another way of manipulating me ("These religious wankers are so vain and stupid they'll believe anything"). What I do know is that in that moment we were able to be free of our mutual prejudices. In that moment, a spontaneous dialogue began beyond our roles—his as capitalist Conquistador and mine as Sacred Activist scourge.

Unconditional love and forgiveness of others are not only for saints and Buddhists. Until you try, you will never explore your own capacity to love and forgive. The sublime courage of the elderly black woman is more accessible to us than we think, once we have the heart-intelligence to realize we need it and the humility to ask the Divine to help us realize it. One of the things life has persuaded me of is that we are all capable of both greater destructiveness and greater heroism than we dare to imagine.

In the story of the black woman in South Africa, I gave an example of the Love Power of Sacred Activism. The second story penetrates to the core of what the Wisdom Power of Sacred Activism can accomplish. It took place in South America in the spring of 1998. I first encountered it in the manuscript of a superb book by Philip Shepherd, *New Self, New World*, which quoted this account from the London *Daily Telegraph*.

Rainforest heroes
Indians' mysterious ritual ends threat of catastrophe

RIO DE JANEIRO – Kukrit and Mati-I are the new heroes of the rain forest. It took the illiterate Kaiapo tribesmen from the Mato Grosso half an hour of mysterious ritual on a riverbank this week to break a five-month drought in the northern Amazon region of Roraima, which had been turned into an inferno.

Their ancestral powers ended what was rapidly turning into one of the world's largest ecological disasters.

Within hours, torrential tropical downpours had put out over 90 percent of the huge jungle fires that had run out of control and destroyed thousands of acres of savannah and rain forest in an area the size of Wales over the past two weeks.

Kukrit and Mati-I—they are unsure about their age as tribal forest Indians count only up to two, all the rest is "very much"—were flown from their tribal village 2,400 kilometres away from the government's Indian Foundation. It was a desperate act which defied all the latest technology and white man's science. The official forecasts were gloomy. Data sent by channel 2 of the NOAA-14 weather satellite and interpreted by the high-tech computers at the Brazilian space center in Jose dos Campos, thousands of kilometres away in the far south of the country, indicated rain in the region was still "at least two to three weeks away."

Hundreds of firefighters were engaged in a hopeless battle against the advancing flames. United Nations emergency aid was offered and considered, army helicopters were dropping "water bombs"—all to no avail. Enormous tracts of virgin rain forest were being devoured and no one could stop it.

Kukrit and Mati-I were unperturbed by their first flight. After they had crossed hundreds of kilometres of jungle they settled in a three-star hotel in Boa Vista, capital of Roraima state in the extreme north of Brazil, took a shower and had a leisurely dinner. Then they went out to the banks of the nearby Curupira River, carrying cipo leaves and taquara branches from their homeland. They were worried that their tribal brothers of the local Yanomami nation would be "eaten" by the flames. "We will make water fall," they promised as they asked to be left alone to perform their ceremony in the dark.

Satisfied, they returned to their hotel 30 minutes later and went to bed, a novelty to them as they are used to hammocks. "It will rain," was all they said before sleeping.

Less than two hours later, the first reports came through on the radio at the army fire task emergency center in Boa Vista. "It started raining here," an almost incredulous voice said from the jungle town of Cacarai.

An hour later, similar reports came in from Apiau, in the region between the Surunu and Majari rivers in the north. When dawn broke, Boa Vista was hit by one of the heaviest downpours in living memory. People danced in the rain in the streets before breakfast and the airport, closed several times in the past few weeks because of smoke from the forest fires, was shut again—this time because of poor visibility caused by the impenetrable rain curtain.

By the end of the day, 25 millimetres had fallen. Humidity rose back to its "normal" 97-percent level.

Satisfied, Kukrit and Mati-I returned to the Mato Grosso. They did not give an explanation. All they said was that they had talked to Becororoti, a famous ancestor gifted with divine power, who, when he died, went to heaven and was turned into rain.

Anyone reading this astonishing and profoundly amusing account will find herself asking the question: *what could be possible, even at this late hour, if the sacred power manifested by two "illiterate Kaiapo tribesmen" could be harnessed on a massive scale?*

To put it another way, what if instead of continuing in what is clearly a suicidal vision of conquering nature, we decided to be guided into a relationship in which we cooperated mystically with Nature so that Nature could cooperate mystically with us? Could whole sections of devastated land be miraculously restored? Could the weather itself, as in the story, be transformed? Could species be revived and fortified at the very last moment? Would Nature herself guide us, as she has native shamans all over the world, to healing herbs and minerals, to simple and effective cures for our modern diseases? Could the genius of Nature guide us to sources of renewable energy we cannot yet imagine?

When Oppenheimer saw the explosion of the atom bomb in the New Mexico desert, he knew that humanity had reached the most dangerous of all thresholds in its evolution. It had acquired godlike powers of destruction without having the spiritual and ethical wisdom to use them responsibly. In his anguish, Oppenheimer quoted from the Bhagavad Gita, India's ancient divine scripture: "Now I am become Death, the destroyer of worlds."

Looking at the devastation we continue to wreak on our planet with these powers, we can see clearly where our use of them will lead—to human extinction and the extinction of a large part of Nature. Our hubristic passion to play God without being infused with divine compassion, tenderness for all life, and knowledge of the divine laws of harmony can lead only to disaster. Absolute human power, ungoverned by awareness of our responsibility to the whole of creation, does not only corrupt absolutely; it inevitably creates situations in which its own destruction is assured. In the addiction to reason that governs our culture, we remain disastrously ignorant of two related laws that shamanic systems know well—that power exercised without wisdom awakens impersonal forces that will destroy those who manipulate them unknowingly, and that the universe, while profoundly benevolent, protects life by ensuring through an inexorable Karmic law that those who attempt to control it without humility create, over time, their own annihilation.

And yet, even at this late hour, there is a way out. I do not believe that we can simply step away from the enormous powers our technological and scientific "mastery" have given us, but we can transfigure and rededicate them, with potentially transformative results. One of the most hopeful adventures of our time is the respectful conversation, pioneered by the Dalai Lama and others, between mystical and scientific truth. With the discovery by 20th-century physicists of an infinitely mysterious, paradoxical universe in which the consciousness of the observer alters what is observed, the possibility arises of a sacred marriage between scientific endeavor and mystical wisdom. This could lead to what His Holiness has called "a new global heart-mind" in which reason and gnosis, the left and right brains, scientific discovery and the deepest mystical knowledge could be fused, with potentially—to our current way of thinking—miraculous results.

When I interviewed the Dalai Lama during the celebration of his Nobel Peace Prize, I asked him about this marriage and his vision of it. His answer exemplified the wisdom this global heart-mind could offer us. The Dalai Lama said, "As you know, I am fascinated by and devoted to science. I have said again and again that I am willing to throw out any of the beliefs of my tradition that do not agree with the rigorous and exact discoveries of science. For example, my tradition has claimed for two millennia that the world is flat, and this is clearly nonsense. What I am asking from scientists is a comparable openness to mystical reality, to the laws of human evolution, and to the power of awakened consciousness enshrined not only in the Tibetan tradition but in all the authentic mystical traditions. I am convinced that one important step forward for humanity will arrive when scientists and the world in general begin to acknowledge that just as the last 300 years of the scientific revolution have opened up a precise awareness of the outer laws of reality, so the ancient mystical traditions offer us a comparable and precise awareness of its *inner* laws.

"If we can marry the knowledge of the outer sciences with the knowledge and practice of the inner sciences of mystical progress, the entire future of the human race can be transformed. Scientists everywhere are now searching for a unified field theory, a theory that can unite and fuse together our knowledge of the laws of the universe; they have already discovered the power of consciousness to alter and affect what is observed. Imagine what could happen if a group of physicists were humble enough to undergo a rigorous mystical education; a deeper experience of consciousness would reveal the secrets of the 'unified field,' and who can predict what powers of invention and healing that would open to humanity?"

I asked the Dalai Lama if he foresaw any dangers in the marriage he was proposing of the outer and inner sciences. He laughed his famous pealing, childlike laugh. "Of course there are dangers. There are always dangers in a great adventure. The greatest danger is that we would misuse the powers this marriage gives us, as we have so misused the powers scientific discovery has opened. But here again, awareness of the inner sciences can help us. All the mystical traditions that are well aware of the great powers to influence and even transform reality that come with growing consciousness warn of using them out of a conscious or unconscious love of domination and exploitation and not balance, harmony, and compassion."

As the Dalai Lama was speaking, I remembered the afternoon eight years before on which everything I had previously understood about reality was overturned. I was in the main shrine room of a Tibetan monastery in Ladakh participating in a long-life ceremony for Thuksey Rinpoche. I had met Thuksey—a magnificent smiling lion of a man—a year before; written a book about our meeting, *A Journey in Ladakh;* and returned to present him with the manuscript. He couldn't have cared less about what I had written and laid aside my manuscript without glancing at it. His only concern was whether I was beginning to honor the Bodhisattva vows I had taken with him and whether I was truly practicing the practices he had given me.

Like many mystical rituals, the long life ceremony seemed to go on interminably and to be more exotically colorful than effective. I remember feeling bored and at moments superior; how could chanting and the muttering of long-winded mantras and the endless lighting and relighting of butter lamps affect the course of the diabetes that was killing Thuksey Rinpoche? I even found myself pitying the old man whose grandeur of spirit had so deeply moved me. I spent most of my time gazing at the peeling frescoes of the shrine room wall, showing off to myself my knowledge of Buddhist iconography and thinking, without much enthusiasm, about the evening meal of Tibetan tea and dumplings.

Then something astounding happened. At the end of the ceremony, Thuksey Rinpoche had to kneel to the young Drukchen Rinpoche, his pupil, considered to be an incarnation of the medieval Tibetan master Naropa. Everyone held their breath as Thuksey, frail and wheezing, lowered himself unsteadily and prostrated on the floor. Seeing him lying there with his arms outspread constricted my heart with pain. Quite suddenly, with shocking energy, Thuksey Rinpoche stood up, looked at me and the group of Westerners I was sitting with, and laughed. At the moment he laughed, a thunderous sound reverberated around the room. From every side the Tibetan word *Tongpanyid,* which means "emptiness," rang out, as if the entire monastery and the mountain it was built on were exploding with it. For a long moment, the Rinpoche's face seemed to become 30 years younger and ablaze with light.

After the ceremony ended, I went to pray in a cave in the mountains above the monastery. When I returned, it was dusk and I sat on a rock across a valley from the shrine room, gazing down at the Rinpoche's room, which adjoined it, and praying for him with a passion of veneration I had never before experienced. A second "miracle" then occurred. I heard, from all sides, the sound of what seemed like thousands of monks chanting, very softly, but unmistakably. It seemed as if the whole of that mountain world—the rocks, the trees, the wild and glinting stream below, the snow-capped caves above—were all chanting in his honor. As the chanting continued deeply and vibrantly, the rocks in front of me started to shine with the same diamond light that I had seen, momentarily, blazing on the Rinpoche's laughing face.

In the early '90s, when I worked with Sogyal Rinpoche to help write *The Tibetan Book of Living and Dying,* I told Sogyal of this experience. He smiled and said, "Our ancient texts tell us that when a being is a true Buddha and has become emptied of self and so full of the creative power of that emptiness that is always manifesting everything, all things testify to his or her truth and obey his will effortlessly." He said this as casually as if he were describing a walk around a park, then turned on the television to watch the evening news.

In the decades since my experience with Thuksey Rinpoche and my interview with the Dalai Lama, I have come to see more consistently that diamond light of Essential Mind and to have innumerable and unmistakable signs of the power that graces anyone who makes some progress toward liberation. I have also encountered, both in myself and in others, the depth, subtlety, range, and danger of that seduction to power that the Dalai Lama warned me of. While I am far from enlightenment, I have been taken far enough on my inner journey to know three things: the claim the Dalai Lama made for the mystical traditions as "inner sciences," precise in their understanding of the stages and ordeals and revelations of inner progress, is a valid one; great powers flow into us as we empty ourselves of our false concepts and attachments; and these powers could help us in every way to heal and transform our degraded inner and outer worlds. We have come too far as a race to abandon the powers we have acquired: in rededicating them to harmony and balance, and uniting them to the wisdom-powers that the Divine graces its true lovers with, a wholly new level of civilization is possible.

There is an ancient Sufi story that shows the extent of the powers that can be invested in a transformed being and clarifies the sacred condition for their practical use. It was first told to me on a gray winter morning in Paris by the great Rumi scholar, mystic, and translator Eva de Vitray-Meyerovitch, a beloved, if cantankerous, friend of mine, who poured out to me a lifetime's knowledge of both Rumi and the Sufi tradition that shaped him.

"There was an emperor who had a slave he loved passionately and who he believed loved him with his whole self. But the emperor wanted to be certain. So he filled ten rooms with heaps of every kind of treasure imaginable—rubies and emeralds, strands of large black pearls, chests full of gorgeous clothes, magnificently illustrated manuscripts, large leather wallets with deeds in them to palaces and country estates. When the rooms were full of this treasure and the walls of the rooms seemed to glow and vibrate in the radiance of so much splendor, the emperor summoned everyone to his court, all his servants and slaves, and said, 'Today I am releasing you all from my service. You are all at perfect liberty to take anything you want from any of the rooms before you.' Pandemonium broke out. Even the Chief Vizier, normally a rather austere and God-fearing man, started to dance a jig and cram into his pockets as many jewels as they could hold."

Eva, who had a flamboyantly theatrical side to her nature, paused here for dramatic effect and gazed out the window long enough for me to imagine just how ridiculous the Grand Vizier's jig must have looked.

"But the slave whom the emperor loved so did not move," Eva continued. "He stayed where he was, silently, gazing at the emperor, until all the treasure was gone and only he and the emperor were left in a desert of empty rooms. The emperor said quietly, 'And you, Mahmoud, what do you want?' Mahmoud answered the emperor: 'I want you.' After a long, ecstatic silence, the emperor said, 'Because you have loved me for myself alone and not for any of my gifts or any of the powers I could give you, everything that I am and everything that I have is yours."

The advanced mystics of every tradition know the secret this story proclaims—that to the one who chooses the Divine for its beauty and holiness alone, the Divine will in turn grant some part of its all-transforming creative power, and in a way that does not compromise the vessel through which it passes.

The pithiest, most comprehensive revelation of what I am trying to convey here is given to us by Jesus in the Gospel of Thomas. It has always seemed to me far more than a vivid coincidence that in 1945, both the first lethal explosions of nuclear horror at Hiroshima and Nagasaki and the discovery, in a small desert cave near Nag Hammadi in Upper Egypt, of this lost gospel occurred. It is as if at the very moment when humanity was brought face to face with its capacity to be "Death, the destroyer of worlds," so also, in Jesus's vision of what he called the "Kingdom" in the Gospel of Thomas, humanity was shown what could still be achieved if it would only wake up and realize the splendor of its secret divinity. The decades since then have only emphasized more intensely the challenge implicit in this synchronicity. Are we going to go on pursuing the addiction to power that could destroy us, or are we going to take up the challenge of Jesus in the Gospel of Thomas to see that the Kingdom of Divine Presence already burns within us?

The Jesus we meet in the Gospel of Thomas knew human beings who had experienced this and allowed themselves to be transformed as he was could create a new world. What Jesus woke up to and proceeded to enact was this new, abundant, and exuberant life of "Kingdom Consciousness," and he did so not as a savior claiming unique status—the Gospel of Thomas makes this clear—but as a revolutionary pioneer of embodied divinity, a sign of what is possible for all human beings who dare to awaken to the glory of their inner truth and the responsibilities for transformation that it inspires within them.

Anyone who has studied the history of Christianity and surveys the state of the contemporary churches operating supposedly in Jesus's name knows that this extremely radical vision has been betrayed. And yet an unbroken line of mystics who awoke to Christ consciousness—from the early apostles and the Desert Fathers to Saint Francis, Teresa of Avila, Saint John of the Cross, and Jan Van Ruysbroeck—all kept alive the outrageous truth of what Jesus announced both in his words and in his healing miracles.

In the 19th century, when the orgy of reason reached its apogee, both the Russian hermit Saint Seraphim of Sarov and the French priest known as the Curé of Ars shocked a smug and skeptical Western world by enacting, in full view, hundreds if not thousands of healings and other "miracles" for which science had no credible explanation. When the body of the Curé of Ars was dug up in the early 1900s, almost 50 years after his death, it was found to be intact, a stunning sign of the power of spirit to transform matter. And in the 20th century, Thomas Merton, Teilhard de Chardin, and, as we shall see, Father Bede Griffiths were inspired by their growing initiation into the full embodied passion of Christ consciousness to imagine a new future for humanity, a birth on earth of the Divine Human.

In the Gospel of Thomas, Jesus tells us: "The seeker should not stop until he finds. When he does find, he will be disturbed. After having been disturbed, he will be astonished. Then he will reign over everything."

These four short sentences contain, for me, the essence of Jesus's inner teaching to humanity and the essence of that Path of Radical Embodiment that he pioneered. What Jesus has given to all humanity is not a path of union with the Transcendent only, but a path through which the transcendent powers of love and wisdom are embodied in the core of human life. This path is at once the most difficult of all, because it involves a grueling and dangerous descent into the personal and collective shadow, and the most empowering, because if it is taken far and deep, it births a new kind of human being: one whose mind is illumined by gnosis, whose heart is aflame with a sacred passion of compassion, and whose body becomes, over time, the conscious receptacle of divine energy.

Jesus is nothing if not a fierce realist, and his teachings show us clearly the price of such a journey. When Jesus tells us, "And when he finds, he will be disturbed," he is making it clear to all those who try to follow him on the Path of Radical Embodiment that contact with the Transcendent will initially cause chaos in our understanding of ourselves and the world. It will demand that we undertake a Descent into our own and the world's shadow and uncover and become conscious of the personal and collective forces of evil and destructiveness. Before we make the descent, it is essential to make vivid and ecstatic contact with the Transcendent Light first, because it is this contact, and the faith in the grace and protection of the Divine that it brings, that will give the "finder" the dogged passion and naked courage that she will need to undertake the marriage of the Light with every aspect of psychic and physical life.

The reward of such a marriage is that after a "disturbing" Descent, it leads in the end to the "astonishment" Jesus celebrates. It *is* astonishing to discover that the Light not only manifests everything, but lives in and as everything, in the tiniest flea and the greatest whale, in all sentient and seemingly insentient things. It *is* astonishing to discover through the long, patient, difficult work of the Descent that even the most disturbing emotions, when made conscious and acknowledged, can be offered up for divine transformation and can form the basis for a greater fellowship with and compassion for all other human beings who wrestle with the same darkness. Perhaps most astonishing of all is the increasing discovery that in all those who take the Path of Radical Embodiment, the very joints and marrow, muscles , guts, and cells of the body itself can house, enshrine, and progressively incarnate divine love, wisdom, energy, and power.

In the last sentence of Logion (saying) 2, "And then he reigns over everything," Jesus makes clear what the ultimate reward and hope of such a process is—the birth on earth, and in the core of life, and in a body, of a tender, illumined, divine human being. This embodied Divine Human is what the alchemists mean when they speak of the legendary "philosophers' stone." They call this process "the Work" or "the making of the philosophers' stone," and they tell us that when the embodied Divine Human begins to emerge, he discovers that the "stone" multiplies endlessly. In other words, the stone becomes a selfless instrument of divine energies that multiplies in its effects throughout the universe.

This vision of Radical Embodiment that Jesus and the alchemical tradition offer humanity fleshes out the first vision I was given by the Dalai Lama in our conversation in Oslo. In a time as drastic as ours, union with the Transcendent alone, without the Descent that marries the Light to our most chaotic impulses and to the depths of the body, will not and cannot be enough. We have seen throughout human history how mystics of all traditions have used bliss and gnosis as a kind of subtle heroin, as an intoxication that allows them to dismiss the body and all earthly realities as "illusion" and so leave them untransformed.

Two Stories of Sacred Activism

As Satprem writes in *Sri Aurobindo, or The Adventure of Consciousness*: "We have denied the divinity of matter to confine it in our holy places and now matter is taking its revenge. If we accept this imbalance there is no hope for the earth. We will swing from one pole to the other—both equally false—from material enjoyment to spiritual austerity without ever finding our plenitude. We need both the vigor of matter and the fresh waters of the spirit."

The marriage the Dalai Lama spoke of—and that Jesus describes and Satprem calls for—between our left and right brains, between the outer and inner sciences, between the vigor of matter and the fresh waters of the spirit, between body and soul, can only take place through a descent into everything that disturbs this marriage in ourselves and in the world. The great hope that we discover if we dare follow this path is that this union of opposites, although difficult, frustrating, bewildering, and sometimes painful, is not impossible; the great birthing energies and incessant grace of the Divine Light itself guide, protect, sustain, and nourish us through everything.

To discover and live this embodied truth is worth every suffering and every ordeal. It is the secret gift, even the purpose, of the crisis we are all living through together. The greatest darkness constellates the most powerful answering light; the greatest threat constellates the most impassioned energy of creativity. When Jesus speaks in the Gospels of the "peace beyond understanding," he is referring not to a passive peace, but to a dynamic peace, a peace beyond any rational explanation or ground that grows as the contraries of light and dark, masculine and feminine are increasingly integrated within us.

Let us imagine together now what humble, divine human beings, born into this marriage of peace and passion, could effect as instruments of God in the world. Imagine what scientists, lawyers, doctors, therapists, politicians, economists, and activists of all kinds could effect as embodied and illumined instruments of compassion and justice. Imagine what illuminations and discoveries of every saving kind would stream through us, not only to preserve human and animal life on earth, but to transform our ways of being and doing everything in every realm—from politics to economics to all arts and sciences.

This is the future that our crisis is invoking for us. What must happen now is that millions of us must be awakened by the growing disaster of our own making to understand that the way forward is, as Jung said, the way *through*—through a naked acknowl-edgment of our collective responsibility for our actions and of the addictions and lust for power that propelled them. If we make a conscious connection with the Divine Light and its grace, we will not only help preserve ourselves and nature, but also transform into spiritually conscious, humble co-creators of an increasingly just and peaceful world.

This is the future that the Divine within and without is pre-paring for us in the crucible of an exploding crisis that is at once a death of all our illusions about ourselves and a potential birth of an embodied Divine Love and Wisdom in us. Our hope lies in seeing this potential clearly and in undergoing joyfully and with faith the ordeals necessary to incarnate it—a hope more powerful and, in Jesus's words, more "astonishing" than any that has yet guided, inspired, or infused us.

CHAPTER 4

THE MESSAGE
OF FATHER BEDE
GRIFFITHS

One of the greatest mysteries of the path is that the Divine will guide you to meet, at the time when you are ready and receptive, the beings who can lead you forward. As Rumi wrote: "The lovers are never abandoned by Destiny; Destiny will unveil to them the sign they will need and hold out to them, in a golden cup, the wine they are thirsty for."

I would never have begun to imagine the evolutionary transformation I am describing, let alone believe in it as the great hope for humanity, had I not met in India, only 50 miles from the place where I was born, a person who incarnated it: Father Bede Griffiths. The great life and work of this brilliant and humble man remains little known, yet for those who were given the grace to meet him, Father Bede is a sign that the birth of the Divine Human is possible.

The tall, gaunt, radiant man I met in his tiny hut when he was 85 and I 41 was not only a great mystic and teacher but also a being clearly undergoing what the Greek Orthodox mystics call "theosis," a subtle transfiguration of the human by the Divine. Father Bede knew this, and in the course of our conversations he described this holiest of transformations with a simplicity and humility that continues to inspire and instruct me. He was not in any way a guru or someone who claimed omniscience or perfect enlightenment. In fact, one of his greatest gifts to me was that he smiled at such pretensions and said again and again, "When, through grace, you are taken to one horizon of Awakening, another, even vaster, opens up before you. Even the highest angels are evolving, drawn ever upward in a passion of love for love." Father Bede was at once the most awe-inspiring and the humblest man I have ever known. It was his humility, in fact, that was the most awe-inspiring thing about him.

He was also extremely funny, as are all the authentically holy people I have met. Like the Dalai Lama, whose divine sense of mischief seems to bubble up in even the direst circumstances, Father Bede's sober majesty of mind was tempered and softened by a delight in human foibles and a compassionate mockery of his own and others' vanity, folly, and self-righteousness. "God save us all from self-righteousness," he once said. "The greatest block to being good is believing you are." His 40 years in India had opened him to the depth of all the mystical traditions, which he had come to see and know as different rays of the same sun of infinite love. The Dalai Lama, who met and loved him, said of him, "Father Bede Griffiths is an awakened being opening the hearts and mind of humanity to gain understanding and acceptance of all the major religions."

I came to meet Father Bede because I was invited by a friend. My friend wanted to make a documentary about him, and I was to be the interviewer who would help guide Father Bede through an account of his long life and unfolding understanding. For ten unforgettable days, I had the honor of inviting Father Bede to share all the different stages of his journey.

On that last morning of filming, Father Bede was calm and collected. After a few moments of small talk, he leaned forward and took my hands. The conversation that followed planted the seeds of everything I have lived and tried to communicate since.

"You know, Andrew, don't you, that we are now living in the Hour of God?"

I was a little startled by his sudden intensity, but answered with a question: "What exactly do you mean by the 'Hour of God'?"

Bede smiled at my Oxford-don tone and then continued.

"I mean that humanity has come to the moment when it will have to choose between trying to play God, with the catastrophic results we see all around us, and trying to become what all the true mystical traditions know we can become—one with God through grace in life. This is a dangerous and yet wonderful and hopeful moment because if enough of us can choose the latter, the birth of a wholly new kind of human being, and so of a new world, is possible."

He paused to let the full impact of what he was telling me sink in. Then he said, "I think that, realistically, there are three possible outcomes to our predicament. The first is that the human race, seeing what a disaster it has gotten itself into through its own folly, will fall on its knees, ask for help, receive it, and be suddenly and astonishingly transformed. This is highly unlikely. Human beings change slowly, and even in desperate circumstances cling to their pride and ignorance. God knows I have.

"The second possibility is that the human race could prove so addicted, confused, and stubborn that it continues on its suicidal course until the bitter end and destroys itself and a large part of nature. There are days for all of us when this appears likely, but this, I am more and more certain, despite all kinds of evidence to the contrary, is an illusion. You see, Andrew, the God that I have come increasingly to know and meet is a God of infinite love, infinite mercy, and infinite resourcefulness. I have been rescued again and again from the worst in myself; even my worst mistakes and stupidest and most destructive thoughts and actions have turned out to create, through some mysterious paradox, doors into deeper compassion for all beings and into action born from this compassion.

"There is a third possibility for the future, and this I am inclined to believe is the one both most likely and in the end most hopeful." Here Father Bede paused again. Then he closed his eyes for a long moment, in which he seemed to be praying for the most exact, most balanced words to express what he was coming to understand.

"What I have come to believe is that the very depth and extent of our crisis is calling forth an unprecedented force of transformation and healing that, if we can align ourselves with it, can not only help humanity survive but also transfigure it. I did not come to this vision through prayer and meditation alone, or even through revelation. I came to it through a profound shattering, almost death, that opened, through grace, into a far more abundant life than any I could have imagined.

"On January 25, 1996, I was sitting meditating as I usually do at 6:00 on the verandah of my hut and suddenly without any warning a terrific force came and hit me on the head. It seemed to be coming from my left and to pull me out of my chair. It was terrifying. I had had a stroke.

"For the next week, I'm told, I didn't speak at all. I can't recall anything of what happened in that week. Then I began to come round. I woke up at about 1:00 one morning, and I thought I was going to die. I decided to prepare for death, so I said the prayers, the normal prayers, and invoked the angels and waited for death. Nothing happened. Then after an hour or two my old friend Christudas, who has been with me for many years, came along and massaged me lovingly, and I begin to get back to something like normal.

"I had some breakfast, and then I felt acutely restless and disturbed and bewildered. I had no idea what was happening; it was as if my whole being had become chaos. Then, quite suddenly, as suddenly in its way as the Force that had felled me, the inspiration came to surrender to the Mother. It was utterly unexpected; I heard a kind of inner voice say loudly, 'Surrender to the Mother,' and so, somehow, I really don't know how, I made a surrender to the Mother. Then I had what I can only describe as an experience of being invaded and overwhelmed by love. Waves of love flowed into me. Judy Walters, my great friend, was watching. I called out to her, 'I'm being overwhelmed by love.'

"What I see now is that this whole experience—from the Force that felled me, through the plunging of my being into chaos, to the ecstasy of being overwhelmed by love and the consciousness that was born from it—was one vast miraculous healing, a divinely orchestrated breakthrough into the dimension of the Divine Feminine. I imagined that I had begun to understand, at least in some fashion, the mystery of the Mother, but I see now I was still very masculine and patriarchal and had been developing my animus all this time; even through all the other inspirations and revelations that grace had given me, I had lived largely in the left brain.

"What happened in that stroke on the verandah was that the right brain—the Divine Feminine, the chthonic power—came and hit me and struck down my left brain in such a way that I could be flooded with the beauty and passion of the feminine I had repressed or denied. Through it, my being was opened to the radiance of the Mother alive in every tree, plant, rock, and sentient being and, increasingly and wonderfully, in the depths of the very body I had tried so long to master and transcend.

"The consciousness I am being brought into now is unlike anything I experienced up until the time of my stroke. It is an increasingly non-dual consciousness in which I experience a profound and mysterious unity with everything and everyone. And it is not intellectual or even 'spiritual' in the old way; it is embodied. My whole being and my whole body are becoming subtly awake in it. Distinctions are not lost in this awareness; everything and everyone, in fact, becomes more individual, sacred, precious, and holy because I am being brought more and more to see that every single sentient being and every pebble and fern and fish is a unique creation of the Divine Light, infinitely loved and cherished, and entirely inhabited by the Light."

Bede fell silent again and birdsong from a nearby tree filled the hut. I struggled to say something, but Bede put his finger to his lips. "I want to now bring together, as far as I am able, everything I have been trying to describe to you about the possibility for the human future and this birth of the Divine in matter. I have come to believe that they are inextricably interconnected, that the Birth that is tentatively and fragmentarily beginning in me is destined to happen on a growing scale in humanity. It will, I believe, happen in you, and it may well be happening, as we speak, to thousands of people all around the world. God is everywhere working a massive Resurrection and it is the destiny of our time to be the birthing-ground of this Resurrection.

"This birthing of a Divine Humanity on a large scale is the real meaning of what some people call the second coming; the Christ does not need to return as a *person*. Jesus in time and history opened this path for us; now what I believe will happen is that the Christ consciousness, or, if you prefer, the Divine-Love conscious-ness, will be born on a massive scale in hundreds of thousands of people. This is a miracle greater than any 'outer' rescuing by God could ever be. We are going to be rescued from 'within' through a massive alchemical process in which the whole of history will take part as a midwife of the new.

"I began our talk by saying that I believed there were three possibilities for the human future—sudden transformation, which I think we can agree is unlikely, and mass suicide, which I do not believe will happen, although, God knows, matters are growing serious. The third possibility, which my own experience leads me to believe will now manifest in history, will be the Great Healing that leads to the Birth.

"What is going to be very difficult for human beings to accept or manage is that this Great Healing will have to manifest first as an immense crisis or a series of immense crises. The force that felled me on the verandah will, I believe, manifest in human his-tory and do to all previous human agendas what it did to mine—plunge them into a cauldron of chaos. This is not punishment, but rescue; not 'damnation' or the 'Last Judgment' or what the funda-mentalists mean by the apocalypse, but the fiercest and most mer-ciful grace. The condition for the glory and possibility of the Birth is a necessary death of all previous visions and ways of acting. In fact, 'Death' and 'Birth' are two sides of one transformation, as I have tried to describe, and are, if you like, 'exploding' together. Out of this 'explosion' within the cauldron of chaos will come a new order, which we can have glimpses of but cannot completely foresee or understand.

"What is essential to surviving, embracing, and being trans-formed by so potentially difficult, dangerous, and bewildering a process is to ground yourself in the hope that the mystical traditions give us through their revelation of our non-dual identity with the Divine and through their knowledge that the Divine works in us and in history in paradoxical ways, using all so-called opposites together to serve its secret alchemy of resurrection. All the traditions know perhaps the most sacred mystery of all—that for the Divine Consciousness to be installed in a human being, that human being has to undergo a death while in the body—a death to his or her false self, to the tyranny of his or her ego and unacknowledged shadow. This death is known in different forms in all the authentic traditions. And of course it mirrors in the inner dimension exactly what happens in outer nature, which recreates itself endlessly through an intricate dance of Death and Birth. If the ear of corn does not 'die' in the dark depths of the soil, the corn does not rise in golden abundance. Shamans know this law. The Sufis know that the lover, to be one with the beloved, has to pass through 'fana,' which some translate as 'annihilation' but I prefer to think of as 'deconstruction of the false self.' Those Christian mystics who have truly begun the journey into embodying Christ consciousness speak of this ordeal as 'the dark night of the soul.' Knowing this mystery and that it ends, not in annihilation, but in the birth of the Divine in matter, in the body, is the clue, I believe, to human survival and the greatest imaginable source of hope."

We heard shuffling and coughing outside the door. The film crew had been patiently waiting for our conversation to end.

I excused myself briefly and went down to the Cauvery River that glittered like molten gold in the already blazing morning sun. I found myself both profoundly shocked and more elated than I had ever been, unable yet to take in what Father Bede had said, but full of gratitude for everything he had given me and certain that nothing in my life would ever be the same.

A week after this conversation took place, back in Paris where I was living at the time, I heard the news that Bede had suffered two strokes and was dying. What he had told me on the last day of filming had already begun to transform my understanding of the human future. To learn that the holy man who had given me that gift was dying, and so soon after our meeting when he had seemed, for all his old age, to be in the greatest of health, devastated me. I knew that I had to go back to India immediately to be with him and be of whatever help or comfort I could. I could not bear to go on with the work he had entrusted to me without seeing him one last time. Our hearts and our beings had so merged in the days we spent together that I felt a part of myself was dying too.

I emptied my bank account, bought a round-trip ticket, and was by Bede's bedside within four days. He was in a terrible state. One side of his body was paralyzed and part of his mind—the intellectually brilliant part—had been largely shattered. Yet for all the horrible pain he was enduring, he was also, for long moments, in a state of grace, overflowing with love for all around him. The strokes had removed the last traces of English reserve; he would hold the hands of his disciples and friends and weep with joy, gazing into their eyes with pure and luminous wonder and childlike trust.

I wrote in my notebook: "In our last conversation before filming ended, Bede talked of his own Dark Night and of the world's, and of how the Dark Night, painful and protracted as it might sometimes seem, is still only a prelude to a Birth that transcends it and transmutes its suffering into peace and bliss. Now, in the agony of his dying, I see Bede himself being born yet again. And his dying is birthing all those who love him, birthing us into an even deeper love for him and so into a deeper revelation of what true communion between souls and loving bodies can reveal."

On the last night I was with him, I sat alone in the early hours of the morning, watching by his bedside as he tossed and turned in an uneasy half-sleep. I drank in every detail of his hands and shoulders and thin powerful chest, every wrinkle of his wracked and exhausted face.

At around 2:00, Bede awoke, reached for my hand, and caressed it. Then, quite suddenly, as if commanded by someone I could not see or hear, he sat up naked in his bed and said loudly over and over again: "Serve the growing Christ! Serve the growing Christ! Serve the growing Christ!"

The Message of Father Bede Griffiths

His words went through me like a sword of light. Everything he had said to me in our conversation in the hut was now crystallized in these four simple words that I experienced as a direct transmission by Divine Love itself. And through the grace of what Bede had said to me and the grace pouring down on us both in that moment, I knew that "serve the growing Christ" meant that our terrible and wonderful time was the destined birthing ground of the Divine Human, the "growing Christ." I knew that anyone who would be brought by the grace of inner revelation to realize this truth would be called upon to do three related things—to serve the growing Christ in himself through meditation, prayer, and surrender to the Divine; to serve all other beings as "growing Christs"; and to serve the "growing Christ" in history through sacred action.

Father Bede Griffiths died five months later after a long agony. I heard of his death in Big Sur, California, one May afternoon. I went down to the sea, put my head in my hands, and wept with loss and relief that his suffering had ended. Then I heard a soft, amused, and unmistakable English voice say to me quite audibly, "Andrew, enough! Look up!" Stunned, I obeyed and saw the sun blazing in a cloudless sky above the sea, streaming, it seemed, a pathway of light directly toward me. The voice went on and said simply, "Do not grieve. I am not dead. The lovers of the One cannot die. I am a ray of the Eternal Sun. I will always be with you."

I told no one what I had experienced, believing it to be a hallucination. The next week, sitting in my study in San Francisco, I came across a passage in one of Rumi's letters that I had never noticed before: "When our guides and those who are cherished by us leave and disappear, they are not annihilated. They are like stars that vanish into the Sun of Reality. They exist by their essence and are made invisible by their attributes. This subject has no end; if all the seas of the world were ink and all the trees of all the forests were pens and all the atoms of the air were scribes, still they would not describe the unions and reunions of pure and divine souls and their reciprocal loves."

Six months later, I became friends with an eccentric Romanian psychic who had been trained personally by Padre Pio and whose

clairvoyant powers dumbfounded me. Before meeting her, I had
been skeptical of psychics, but seeing her at work had convinced
me of her gifts. One afternoon she rang me and said, "Don't ask
me what this means, but a very old smiling English man dressed
in what looked like orange curtains came to me and said he had a
message for you. The message was 'What happened by the sea in
California was more than illusion.' Have you any idea of what this
might signify?" For a long time I couldn't say anything. Then I
asked her if I could ring her back later, and I put the phone down.
The film company that my Australian friend had cobbled together
to film the documentary on Father Bede was More than Illusion
Films. Bede had confirmed for me the immortality of the soul by a
very Oxford kind of joke.

From this experience, I started to realize that the Birth into
Divine Love never ends but goes on and on expanding. I began
to understand, too, that death is only a changing face of Eternal Birth, the mode and means by which it incessantly recreates
and resurrects itself, and there is no end, in any universe or realm
imaginable, to the wonderful alchemies that Love can reveal. The
unfolding joy and hope born from this realization are Bede's greatest gifts to me.

After I left Bede's deathbed, my life was forever altered. The
reordering force of Bede's grace was immediate. When I returned
to Paris, I met the young man who was to become my husband.
And then my world fell apart and my life was plunged into a prolonged Dark Night. My then-guru, ordered me to leave my beloved,
marry a woman, and write a book (following the one I had already
written about her) claiming that her divine force had transformed
me into a heterosexual. After a terrible struggle, I realized that in
order to live my life I would have to not only leave my guru, but
also announce to the spiritual world what she had done. It was my
early witness that had brought many people to her. It was now my
duty to speak out, whatever the consequences.

Had I not been prepared both by Father Bede and by my own
study of the mystical tradition for the rigors of the Dark Night, I
would have gone mad. The intense suffering of being betrayed by

a guru I had loved with all my heart and soul was compounded by the heartbreak of being abandoned by old friends, being terrified by repeated death threats, and feeling grief-stricken by the cancer my husband developed under the stress of what happened. Bede had said that the worst suffering of all is to believe your pain is meaningless. What Bede had told me and what I had read in Rumi's poetry helped me keep faith when everything I knew and trusted was being shattered. Thanks to Bede and the understanding of this process in both Christian and Islamic mysticism, I knew I was being killed to be reborn. That helped me to go on believing, trusting, and hoping, even as events brought me repeatedly to my knees.

Devastating though this experience of the Dark Night was, it was also profoundly beautiful and transforming. I came to know, in my deepest being, that the process of the Dark Night is in itself an extreme marriage of opposites. On the one hand, the process burns down, destroys, and undoes the false self. On the other, it opens up the real self to wholly new levels of sacred passion and intimate knowledge of the Divine.

The greatest gift of the Dark Night I was living through was that it radicalized me. It turned me from a mystic obsessed with the inner world into someone actively involved in changing the structures of society and the ways in which power is distributed and exercised. In a prolonged and frightening way, the corruption of one accepted system of power—that of the guru system and its advocates—made me far more sensitive than I had ever been before to the ruthless effect of power in general. The connections between all systems of domination, religious, political, and economic, began to be painfully clear to me, not just intellectually but also viscerally. I began to understand, not just with my mind but also with my heart and guts, that these very systems that rule our religions and corporations and political parties are what keep us radically disempowered, paralyzed, and depressed.

Through the Dark Night, all separation between religion and politics becomes meaningless because you see with clarity that all the cruelty, madness, and injustice "out there" are emanations from a collective false self dangerously out of control. Two things help you bear this new level of radical exposure to reality—a far greater intensity of inner experience in which the divinity of every being, flower, dog, and flea burns steadily before you and a naked and fierce commitment to help others, whatever happens. These gifts come together; they are the wild graces of the Dark Mother— the force of the Divine Feminine that felled Father Bede—and the golden fruit that matures in the pain of the Dark Night. The Dark Mother kills you and rebirths you into her dimension of boundless love. And when that love is felt in its heartbreak and in its joy, in its despair and in its hope, in its great peace and in its great passion, it turns you from believing that spirituality is a private process to knowing that love means nothing unless it is put into action for compassion and justice.

CHAPTER 5

THE VOICE
OF THE FIRE

Several years later, the Divine intervened again in my life to break it open further and reveal to me more deeply what my work had to be.

My mother sent me a fax from Coimbatore, the place in India where I was born, to say that my father was in the hospital, dying, and that I needed to come immediately if I wanted to see him. Within three days I was at my father's bedside. The first time I saw him, he was still as I had always known him, handsome and regal, but also visibly harrowed by the combination of kidney and heart failure. I knew he was dying. None of the differences, political or otherwise, that had sometimes separated us meant anything now. All that mattered was the love and respect that had always been the truth of our relationship.

Every morning I would spend a couple of hours with him, holding his hand; dabbing his brow; stroking his shoulders; talking to him when he wanted to talk; and telling him again and again how much I loved him and how much I admired him, how grateful I was that he was my father, and how my vision of what it is to be a man was rooted in his passion for justice, in his dignity, and in the decency he had never failed to show me and all those he loved.

When my father could speak, he would tell me how much he believed in the difficult work I was trying to do. "Never give up," he said, "whatever they say about you or do to you. You do not come from rich or powerful people, but you come from God's own people, a line of soldiers and priests, a line of people who trust in God and God's guidance, come what may. This is the blood that runs in my veins and it is the blood that runs in yours. I have been so frightened for you. I knew your nature would take you into wild waters and that neither I nor anyone else would be able to protect you. Trust in the protection of God and go forward humbly. All that will matter when you lie dying, as I am now, is knowing that you gave what you could to help others and that you are loved, not for what you have and not even for what you have done, but for what you are."

I had spent half a lifetime wandering the world to seek out sages who could teach me the wisdom I hungered for. Now I realized that in my father, whom I had sometimes inwardly patronized, I had always had the finest of teachers, one who taught not through words but through a subtle and humble presence that moved everyone he met.

Most of our conversation in that magical and holy week was about Jesus. In those precious hours by his bedside, my father stunned me with the depth of fervor and intense simplicity of his Christian faith and his trust in Jesus, whom he called "my friend and my brother." I had known many things about my father, his passion for gray and subdued green in clothes, his preference in cologne and shaving brushes, his love of historical biographies. But until that last week together I had never understood how everything he did, everything he was, emanated from the ground of his faith. I came to understand that the gentlemanliness that characterized him even when he was in grief or suffering was far more than social conditioning or the "best of Britishness." It arose from a commitment to a courtesy of soul, a fundamental respect for all beings, whatever their status or sexuality or religion or nationality.

One night I asked my father as he lay white and worn out from the night's anguish, "Which Jesus are you praying to now?" With a smile, he said simply, "I am praying to my friend as he was in Gethsemane because it was then that he needed help and I need help now."

As the days went by, I shared with my father what I had learned from Father Bede and the message he had given me. I told him what had happened with my guru and during the long ordeal afterward. My father told me how he had come to see that the future of the world was in danger and that only a revolution of the heart expressed in action could now transform the situation. "I hope to God we still have time," he kept saying. "I pray every day that we still have time." It moved me deeply that even as he was dying, my father, in his pain, opened more and more profoundly to the world's suffering. He told me often how much he loved his grandchildren and how anguished he was at the future they were facing. "You must do everything you can to see that they stay strong. Go on living your life in faith so they can see that faith gives you courage and power and hope and energy to go on doing everything you can to be of help."

I arrived in Coimbatore on a Tuesday. That Sunday I went with my younger brother, who had flown to India also, and with old family friends to the services at a local Catholic church. It was the feast day of Christ the King. The church was full of marigolds and roses, Indian worshippers in their flamboyant and sweet-smelling best, little girls with silk ribbons and jasmine in their hair, and distinguished, gaunt old men and mothers and grandmothers in crisp red and gold saris. An old man in horn-rimmed glasses that flashed in the sun read the Gospel from Matthew 25:31–40. If I had to choose one passage from all the world's scriptures that expresses the essence of the truth I have come to believe, it would be this one. And on that Sunday, I heard each word afresh, as if for the first time, with a broken-open heart:

the heart breaks open

49

When the Son of Man shall come in his glory, and all the holy angels with him, then shall he sit upon the throne of his glory:

And before him shall be gathered all nations: and he shall separate them one from another, as a shepherd divideth his sheep from the goats:

And he shall set the sheep on his right hand, but the goats on the left.

Then shall the King say unto them on his right hand, "Come, ye blessed of my Father, inherit the kingdom prepared for you from the foundation of the world:

"For I was hungered, and ye gave me meat: I was thirsty, and ye gave me drink: I was a stranger, and ye took me in.

"Naked, and ye clothed me: I was sick, and ye visited me: I was in prison, and ye came unto me."

Then shall the righteous answer him, saying, "Lord, when saw we thee hungered and fed thee? Or thirsty, and gave thee drink?

"When saw we thee a stranger, and took thee in? or naked, and clothed thee?

"Or when saw we thee sick, or in prison, and came unto thee?"

And the King shall answer and say unto them, "Verily I say unto you, Inasmuch as ye have done it unto one of the least of these my brethren, ye have done it unto me."

The old man sat down, and a small, smiling, plump Indian priest took his place and began his sermon. As he spoke of India's poverty and the growing sufferings of the planet, the tiny priest's voice swelled and shook. He said that Jesus is the mystical King of the universe, not because of his miracles, not because he walked on water or raised the dead, not even because he left us such teachings as Matthew 25, but because again and again he gave himself away to human beings out of a supreme, inextinguishable, and fiery love that no cruelty could deter and even the most humiliating death imaginable could not defeat. It was this fiery passion of love, the priest went on to say, that resurrected Jesus. It is this passion of love that will resurrect the world from its suffering and poverty, despair and apathy.

I felt as if I was hearing the essential message of Jesus's life to all human beings for the first time, almost as if Jesus himself were telling it to me.

After the priest finished talking and sat down, I looked up at the statue of the resurrected Christ at the end of the church. The only thing I can say about what happened next is that the statue became alive. For almost 15 minutes I saw the Christ in majestic, radiant golden light. No human words could ever convey what that moment was like. It was both an ecstasy and an agony beyond anything I had ever known or even imagined, an ecstasy of rapture, amazement, gratitude, and adoration and an agony at what seemed like a knife plunging again and again into my chest. When the knife of light had finished its work, I saw how my own slashed-open heart flowed back to him in an answering molten stream of fire. Love, lover, and Beloved were all one in grace. All were one all-transforming fire of divine, passionate compassion. As this fire streamed between my heart and the heart of the resurrected Christ, I knew that what Divine Grace was giving me was not only an ineradicable revelation of the cosmic force of Divine Love but also an experience of my own innermost truth, my own embodied human divinity and that of all human beings who would allow themselves to be possessed and transformed by Divine Passion. I knew that the fire streaming between my heart and the Christ's was the fire that would birth a new world out of the Death of our crisis, a fire that would enable those wild and brave enough to survive its ordeals—once they discovered it in their own inmost being—to burn with unconditional compassion, joy, and passion for justice through all the coming cataclysms. This was the fire in which a new world would be created out of the smoldering ashes of the old; this was the fire that would burn in the heart of a transformed humanity and give it the energy to reinvent all institutions, arts, and sciences in the name of Love and Justice.

The experience, however, did not end with that vision and its revelations. As I stumbled out of the church into the humid, scalding ferocity of an Indian noon, I saw beside the open gate of the church an emaciated young man. He must have been around 25, with no arms or legs, planted in a filthy puddle. He was one of the most beautiful human beings I have ever seen, with a face seared and honed by distress and humiliation. As I ran toward him to gather him up in my arms and help him out of the puddle and place whatever money I had in his pocket, he looked up at me. As his eyes burned into mine, I knew that just as I had seen the Christ in glory in the statue in the church, now I was seeing the Christ in this armless and legless man, crucified by suffering and poverty.

A voice within me then began to speak. It was so loud I was almost deafened by it, although no one else heard it. *You have been playing with Light all these years that you believed you were making spiritual progress. You have been exploiting the mystical teachings and experiences you have been given for yourself, your career, your own self-ish delight. Don't you understand that the purpose of everything you have been through is to make you a servant of Divine Love in action in the world? Don't you realize that if grace has opened up the divine realms to you, it is so that you can be devoted and humble enough to dedicate all of your thoughts and emotions and actions and resources to the ending of the horror that you see before you? The world is burning to death in the fires of greed and ignorance. All of animal and human life is now threatened. This being that you see before you is one of billions in anguish. See behind him and around him the burning forests, the polluted seas, the vanishing tigers and polar bears. The Divine is being crucified again and again by a humanity obsessed with its own needs and driven increasingly by a crazed and suicidal hunger to dominate and control and exploit everything. Everything you are and everything you do from this moment on must help human beings awaken to their inner divinity and to its responsibilities of urgent sacred action. The only questions you will be asked when you cross over the waters of death are "What did you do while the world was burning? How did you work to heal the horror of a world on fire? What did you love enough to risk and give your life for?" Nothing else will matter. Understand this now.*

The Voice of the Fire

Turn away from everything you have been and done and believed, and dive into the furnace of a Divine Love that embraces all beings. Give your whole life to spread and embody the message of its passion to the world—that the world must now wake up, claim the sacred fire that lives within every human heart, and act from it. The one hope, both for you and for humanity, is to take up the challenge of the Divine and put the fire of Divine Compassion into radical action in every arena of the world.

The ferocity and ruthlessness of this inner voice terrified me. It left me nowhere to turn and no self-justification to cling to. I felt vulnerable, naked, broken, and exposed, a fraud and fool, absolutely inadequate to what was being asked of me, afraid of what the voice was revealing to me about the situation of the world.

What I had already lived through in the years after I left my guru had almost killed me. What would I now risk, stepping forward, as the voice demanded, to spread and embody love in action? How much more would I have to endure? With all the faults and neuroses of my nature, which the Beloved had so fiercely revealed, how would I be able to do His work without risking my life and eternal soul? Would the ingenious narcissist in me be able to twist even this message to suit its ends? How could I begin to trust myself after what I had been shown so ruthlessly about myself? I knew that I had been given, in this time while my father was dying, in the place where I was born, a grace that would forever change my life and focus its direction and purpose. But a part of me longed to refuse and deny it even as I knew its truth.

The dull brutality of my ungrateful selfishness made me reel with despair. If I, who had pursued spiritual truth for 20 years, could be so resistant to a vision that I knew came directly from the Divine, how would others whose belief in God was shaken by the horrors of a devastated world even begin to receive the message, let alone act upon it? As the waves of awe and revelation started to subside, I was left in a state of helplessness mingled with fury that the Divine was asking of me, and everyone else, something that seemed impossible.

Deep prayer combined with the peaceful presence of my father, to whom I had told nothing of what I had experienced, slowly began to steady me. I began to understand that the shame and disgust I had felt were inevitable and natural. Exaggerating their importance or prolonging them would be yet another game of the ego, another way of defending myself from compassion and forgiveness. The Beloved knew me better than I knew myself. Why would the voice have urged me to embody the message if its grace would not help me do so? I was being asked to trust in God and give and do my best, knowing that I would fail and falter and sometimes make drastic mistakes; knowing, too, that if I continued to try, nakedly and sincerely, and go on and on asking for help and illumination, they would be given, and given with an extravagance of grace that always, despite myself, would carry me forward. I had been taken through death after death to arrive at this tremendous birth in the place where I had been born. I knew that what I needed to be and do would be revealed. My only way forward would be through an ever-renewing and ever-deepening surrender to a mystery I would never understand—whose nature I knew now was unfathomable—and to a fiery, unconditional love, a love beyond reason or comprehension, a passion of Divine Compassion whose energy creates and pervades all living things.

In doing the will of that all-powerful and all-embracing love, however imperfectly, lay my only hope of peace in fulfilling the destiny I had been summoned to. This destiny had nothing to do with any kind of worldly or spiritual success. I had been called not to succeed but to serve come what may, through whatever difficulties, humiliations, or obstacles arose. I was not a prophet, but a servant. The message I was being instructed to give was not mine. Any attempt on my part, even unconsciously, to claim or control it would be a betrayal of its challenge and mercy. Serving it offered me one thing and one thing only: what Jesus meant by "the pearl of great price," the inner certainty that I was fulfilling my life's holiest purpose and the chance to be able to answer the question "What did you do when the world was burning?" Not with a few books, but with the example of my own passionate, flawed devotion in service, helping the world discover the transforming vision of the Birth and its fiery resurrecting force of sacred action.

Four days after the vision in the church, I went into my father's bare hospital room to say a final good-bye to him. There was no sadness between us at our last meeting; to be sad when so much had been given would have been absurd. A great peace enfolded us both, and I realized that I had been and always would be the son of an ordinary and holy man who had served compassion in every way he knew, without vanity or fanfare. Knowing that gave me a deeper faith in myself. I was, after all, his son, flesh of his flesh, and what I so loved in him was also, through the power and blessing of his patient love, in me.

Before I left my father that last time, I knelt by his bedside and, with my head bowed, thanked him for everything he had done and been and given. It was a long list and I did not hurry. When I finished, I looked up at him to see him gazing down at me, his eyes shining with love. "Bless me, father," I said.

He put both his hands on my head and rested them there as he began to speak, quietly at first, but then with gathering power.

"You asked me to bless you and I will. I hope you will live a long and healthy and happy life. I hope you will always be surrounded by love and friends, and I hope you have the money you need to realize your gifts. But those things are not what I am going to bless you with now."

Here he paused a long time and I saw one solitary gleaming tear spill from his right eye. It was the first and last time I ever saw him cry.

"I ask God to be my witness now, and, knowing I only have the authority of my love for you to do so, I bless you with the love and presence of the Christ. May the Christ always be visible to you in your heart. May you always know that the Christ is walking with you, and may you obey whatever the voice in your heart tells you to do and be. Take whatever consequences come with hope and faith and courage and humility."

In his voice, I heard the Beloved challenging me and breaking me open to a life of love in action. I could not speak. I got up, bowed to my father, kissed him, and left the room. I knew I had been given the greatest and deepest blessing a father could give a son, and I knew that the blessing of the Divine Father had come through my father to me.

I returned to America and plunged into years of exhausting touring and teaching and writing. Almost immediately on returning from India, I started to meet others who had received similar messages about the need to put Divine Love into action if the world was to be preserved. A sober businessman from Nebraska told me how the Buddha had appeared to him in a series of dreams and shown him clearly that now everything depended upon compassion and the action that flows from it. A Navajo elder wrote to me after hearing me speak of what I experienced in Coimbatore and shared with me not only his native prophecies but also those of the Mayans, Aztecs, Hopis, and Aborigines, all of which pointed to our age as a time in which the fate of the earth is at stake and we have the chance to bring about a revolution by restoring the ancient knowledge of harmony with nature. A Tibetan lama with whom I had worked while writing *The Tibetan Book of Living and Dying* educated me in detail about the prophecies of the 13th Dalai Lama and Padmasambhava (a great yogi of the 8th century) that predict the collapse of our era, but also point to its potential for extraordinary renewal.

As I continued to tour and teach, the depth and range of the challenge being received now everywhere became clearer to me. I realized increasingly that what I had been put in contact with in Coimbatore was the primordial fire-force of Divine Love known in all authentic mystical traditions: known as Ishq (or divine passion) in Sufism, as Shakti in the Hindu vision, as the Shekinah in Jewish mysticism, and as absolute Bodhicitta in Mahayana Buddhism. The great universal mystic Ramakrishna called this force "Mother's fiery love," and I came to understand that it was this divine fire of passionate compassion that was now going to be embodied in as many human beings as possible in order to transform the world.

The Voice of the Fire

What my vision in Coimbatore and the messages being received by others all over the world confirmed to me was that it was no longer enough to merely feel and know this force, or even to be substantially transformed in its flames. The full intensity of its clarity, purity, and passionate urgency had to be focused on the task of transforming all existing economic, political, and social systems. If this force remained the ecstatic private experience of a few privileged mystics, its true revolutionary power would be drastically tamed. It needed to be activated and brought right into the heart of the burning world. How exactly to activate this force in myself and in others, and how to bring it into the world, became the focus of my days and nights. I meditated constantly on the fire and prayed to be illumined by it.

Then, late one evening, I started to understand that the way the experience unfolded in Coimbatore contained several essential clues.

The experience had begun with a great ecstasy of sacred passion, a lava flow of love between the heart of the Divine and my heart. This revelation of the sacred fire of Divine Love burning in everything was the first step, but it was not enough.

I remembered that in the Arthurian legends, Percival had been graced with the vision of the Grail not because he was braver or more brilliant than his fellow knights, but because he had asked the one crucial question: "What is the Grail for?" (In other versions, it's "Whom does the Grail serve?") The vision I had been given was not for my private liberation alone. What the experience of the sacred fire was "for" was to change the world by changing the beings whom it inspired so that they could become the servants of radical compassion and justice in reality—rebels and revolutionaries of love in action, prepared to risk everything to help the Divine transform humanity.

The door into this empowered servitude, the voice of the fire told me, was through facing the cruelty, the injustice, and the agony of the world head on and letting them shatter the heart open. The detachment and serenity so prized by the old patriarchal mystical systems could not be enough for a crisis so

enormous. The authentic rebel of love would have to let himself
be penetrated and broken open by love. This would be a devastating experience—devastating to the tidy brutalities of the false self,
but devastating also to the more subtle narcissism of the prevailing one-sided visions of enlightenment, which were themselves
the result of an addiction to transcendence.

I knew this addiction very well in myself and saw its dissociation in all those around me. I saw it in Buddhists who, when I
spoke of the need for action in the burning world, told me to calm
down because "everything is emptiness"; in Hindus who wrote to
me and said: "You are becoming much too excited about nothing,
the world is nothing but an illusion"; in New Age fundamentalists who smiled serenely at me and spoke in soft voices about how
"only the light is real and all is always in divine order so there is
nothing to worry about."

The activists I knew were separated in crucial ways from the
ecstasy and power that sacred vision could offer them. Many of
them had rejected the notion of the Divine altogether. This meant
that they were tragically cut off from the inspiring energies of
divine awareness and love, mired instead in a denunciatory, divi-
sive consciousness that created as many problems as it intended to
solve and alienated many of those it longed to enthuse.

Mystics, I saw, were mostly addicted to being, activists to
doing. Both had profound narcissistic shadows that I recognized
in myself. The mystic's shadow was a surreal dissociation from the
body, the world, and the grueling tasks of implementing justice.
The activist's shadow lay in the messiah and martyr complexes
that accompany the addiction to *doing*, with its vulnerability to
burnout, rage, and despair.

One night I dreamed I saw two rivers of flame meet in a sea
of boiling fire and heard these words: "When the two fires meet,
a third fire is created, more powerful than either." When I awoke
and meditated on my dream, I understood that these two fires
were the fire of the mystic's passion for God and the fire of the
activist's passion for justice, and that in the fire I had experienced
in Coimbatore, these two fires were fused. In the greatest of human

beings—Jesus, Rumi, Buddha—and in beings of our own time such as Nelson Mandela, the Dalai Lama, and Martin Luther King, Jr., these two fires were fused in a "third fire"—the fire of wisdom and love in action.

This third fire was, I realized, the key to preparing and transforming the human race. If the fire of the mystic's passion for God could be married to the activist's passion to enact change, then a new kind of human being would be born. This human being would be grounded in universal, all-embracing, mystical truth and would be acting for justice in a local context with a global consciousness, beyond national or tribal or religious boundaries. The mystic's shadow of addiction to being would be healed by the activist's focus on doing. The activist's shadow of addiction to doing would be balanced and transformed by the mystic's surrender to divine wisdom and joy. The fusion of the mystic's passion for God with the activist's passion for justice in one Divine fire would heal the tragic split in our modern consciousness between masculine and feminine, body and soul, light and matter, passion and peace, inner contemplation and outer action.

Such a vision, I knew from my immersion in the world's mystical traditions, was not a wholly new one. It was known in part, in the Rigveda and the core vision of ancient Vedic Hinduism; it was reflected in the evolution of the Bodhisattva ideal in Mahayana Buddhism, and in the vision of the Jewish prophets. Both Eastern and Western systems of alchemy had at their core an image of a being transformed by both internal vision and external action into the ideal they called "the philosopher's stone," a human being humbly radiating divine power and grace.

In the 20th century, this vision of an evolutionary humanity incarnated itself in the brilliant work of Sri Aurobindo, Teilhard de Chardin, Jean Gebser, and in our time, Ken Wilber. Father Bede Griffiths had written about this transformation and lived it. In his wonderful book *Return to the Center,* Father Bede compared the goals of Sri Aurobindo's vision with that of authentic Christian mysticism: "In the integral Yoga of Sri Aurobindo matter and life and consciousness are seen to be evolving toward the divine light and the divine consciousness in which they are not annihilated but fulfilled . . . [T]his is the goal of a Christian Yoga. Body and soul are to be transfigured by the divine light and to participate in the divine consciousness. There is a descent of the spirit into matter and a corresponding ascent by which matter is transformed by the enduring power of the spirit and the body is transfigured.

"There must be a movement of ascent to pure consciousness, a detachment from all the moods of nature, a realization of the self in its eternal ground beyond space and time, but then there must also be a movement of descent by which the spirit enters into the heart of matter and raises it to a new mode of existence in which matter becomes the medium of a spiritual consciousness."

When I read these words for the first time in a decade, not long after I had returned from my father's deathbed, I knew they contained the clue to everything that had been happening within me since I had started on the path. After what I had experienced in South India, it was clear to me that this divinization process was not just for exalted saints and yogis working on their transformation in isolation. It could be the destiny of millions of human beings. The movement of descent that Bede spoke of by which the spirit enters into the heart of matter was not a luxury for a few evolved seekers, but a necessity for humanity as a whole. And if this movement of descent was inspired and clear and directed enough, it would effect a huge evolutionary leap, a new mode of existence for a humbled and transformed humanity dedicated to putting Divine Love into action.

I made many mistakes and suffered many setbacks in the years that followed, and I needed to undergo many more trials, revelations, and ordeals to begin to embody the reality of what I had learned. But four linked realizations have only grown clearer with the passing years: humanity is now undergoing the Death known as the "dark night of the soul"; this Dark Night is not punishment or damnation, but a mystery of fierce transforming grace; as it exposes their illusions and shatters their hearts open, hundreds of thousands of beings all over the world are being reborn into a peaceful passion to put love into action; and Sacred Activism, fuelled by the "third fire" that rises from the marriage of the mystic's passion for God and the activist's passion for justice, is the birthing force for a new humanity.

I feel I have come to know these four linked truths not merely in a spiritual and intellectual way but in a visceral way too. The pain and hope of these truths live not only in my heart and mind and soul but also in my body, and as my knowledge lives more and more in my guts and muscles, my capacity to respond to what I know becomes simpler, humbler, and more effective.

What fills me with hope is that millions of human beings are now, in the fire of our current crises, waking up to the need for inner and outer transformation, making possible the quantum evolutionary leap I have been describing. The time for the Birth of Sacred Activism on a global scale has arrived. Everything is now at stake and everything is possible.

PART II

"Honor the highest truth in the universe: it is the power on which all things depend: it is the light by which the whole of life is guided. Honor the Highest within yourself: For it too is the power on which all things depend and the light by which the whole of life is guided."

— Marcus Aurelius, from "Meditations"

CHAPTER 6

THE FIVE
FLAMES OF THE
SUN OF HOPE

I see the Hope that will guide us out of our darkness and distress as being like a sun with five flames bursting from it. Each flame is both a peaceful and a passionate power of this Hope. Experiencing each separately and then all five together will give you great strength, courage, stamina, and compassion and a profound inner energy that the difficulties and dangers of working to change the world cannot defeat.

In a situation as challenging and volatile as ours, it is essential to imagine and connect with the kind of hope that dangerous circumstances and human frailty cannot distort. It is the great gift of the world's mystical traditions; at the moment when we need it most, their combined wisdom offers us a magnificent and empowering vision, one rooted not in human abilities, but in the nature of the Divine and the essential human relationship with the Divine. At the time of our greatest danger as a human race, the most comprehensive and exalted vision of hope has arisen to give us the strength and joy we will need not only to go forward but also to endure what is necessary for our transformation and for the preservation of our planet.

THE FIRST FLAME: THE NATURE OF GOD

All the authentic mystical traditions tell us, in different words and symbols, that the Divine is One, an all-encompassing and omnipresent Light-consciousness whose absolute nature is joy, peace, and boundlessly creative energy and intelligence. The traditions also agree that this Light-consciousness loves its creations with an infinite tenderness and that it is constantly irradiating, nourishing, sustaining, and transforming all things through grace.

The mystical traditions all tell us that the One keeps birthing the universe through a dance, or "marriage," of opposites. When we are in ordinary egoistic consciousness, we experience these opposites as antagonistic and unrelated. When, however, we are initiated through mystical realization into the One from which they emanate, we begin to become aware of the interconnectedness between them. We become aware, in awe and wonder, that what we thought of as solid matter is in fact concentrated light-energy, that what we have characterized as evil can birth a new level of good, that death is the gate into rebirth, that destruction is a condition for new creation, and that the sufferings we fear can become the ground for a greater compassion.

This growing knowledge of the interconnectedness of seeming opposites births in us, over time, a great joy and profound hope. We come to know that even the worst horrors are part of a larger, richer, more sublime, and mysterious alchemy. Even physical death is only a gate into deeper life.

We come to know and experience, with growing gratitude, the peace and bliss of the One behind all the changing manifestations of its dance. The Hope that springs from this realization cannot be shaken by any horror or anguish; it cannot be defeated by any of the circumstances of human life or human history. It is a hope born from and rooted in the eternally blissful, perpetually creative nature of the One itself.

Many mystics in all traditions have lived in the eternal sunrise of this Hope. The bliss, joy, and promise of this "simple union,"

The Five Flames of the Sun of Hope

with the love beyond all opposites, has never been more beautifully and accurately expressed than by Kabir, the great universal Indian mystic of the 15th century:

O SADHU! the simple union is the best.
Since the day when I met with my Lord, there has been no
 end to the sport of our love.
I shut not my eyes, I close not my ears, I do not mortify
 my body;
I see with eyes open and smile, and behold His beauty
 everywhere:
I utter His Name, and whatever I see, it reminds me of
 Him; whatever I do, it becomes His worship.
The rising and the setting are one to me; all contradictions
 are solved.
Wherever I go, I move round Him,
All I achieve is His service:
When I lie down, I lie prostrate at His feet.

He is the only adorable one to me: I have none other.
My tongue has left off impure words, it sings His glory day
 and night:
Whether I rise or sit down, I can never forget Him; for the
 rhythm of His music beats in my ears.
Kabir says: "My heart is frenzied, and I disclose in my soul
 what is hidden. I am immersed in that one great bliss
 which transcends all pleasure and pain."

Another universal mystic, Rumi, who lived for 30 years in the splendor of this "simple union," wrote of the wonder of what was unveiled to him through it:

The wine of Divine Grace is limitless:
All limits come from the faults of the cup
Moonlight floods the whole sky
From horizon to horizon

> How much it can fill your room
>> Depends on its windows
> Grant a great dignity, my friend,
> to the cup of your life
> Love has designed it to hold his Eternal wine.

The human being who awakens, as Rumi has, to the presence of the Divine Light as the "moonlight" that "floods the whole sky from horizon to horizon" comes simultaneously to know that "the wine of Divine Grace is limitless." This limitless wine of grace is pouring down incessantly, in and through every event, through pain as well as joy, what we call evil as well as what we call good, through ordeal as well as happiness, terror as well as calm. In order to realize this, Rumi makes clear, you have to open wide the windows of your room, open yourself beyond reason and beyond your own small and limited powers of understanding and judgment to allow yourself to experience the Mystery of the One who dances in and for creation *and* destruction, life *and* death. Knowing more and more that you are the Child of the One brings you into the field of a hope that, like the One, transcends all opposites of victory or defeat, triumph or survival.

As Rumi wrote:

> One day in your wine shop I drank a little wine
> And threw off the robe of body
> And knew, drunk on you, this cosmos is harmony
> Creation, destruction I am dancing for them both.

One who dances like that lives in eternal hope and eternal joy.

THE SECOND FLAME:
HUMANITY'S RELATIONSHIP WITH GOD

In the Chandogya Upanishad, one of Hinduism's most inspired scriptures, the realized Brahmin sage Uddalaka reveals the essential secret of the relationship between the human and the Divine when he says to his son, Shvetaketu:

> As by knowing one lump of clay, dear one,
> We come to know all things made out of clay—
> That they differ only in name and form,
> While the stuff of which all are made is clay;
>
> As by knowing one gold nugget, dear one,
> We come to know all things made out of gold—
> That they differ only in name and form,
> While the stuff of which all are made is gold;
>
> As by knowing one tool of iron, dear one,
> We come to know all things made out of iron—
> That they differ only in name and form,
> While the stuff of which all are made is iron—
>
> So through spiritual wisdom, dear one,
> We come to know that all of life is one.
>
> In the beginning was only Being,
> One without a second.
>
> Out of himself he brought forth the cosmos
> And entered into everything in it.
> There is nothing that does not come from him.
> Of everything he is the inmost Self.
> He is the truth; he is the Self supreme.
> You are that, Shvetaketu; you are that.

Each of the major systems has a different way of characterizing this essential, non-dual relationship with the One. Jesus in the Gospels says, "The Kingdom is within you." Black Elk, speaking simply out of the heart of the indigenous wisdom of the world, tells us, "At the center of the universe dwells Wakantanka, and this center is really everywhere and within each of us." The Sufi mystics of Islam proclaim that "the lover and the beloved are one." The mystery of Enlightenment celebrated in Buddhism is the mystery of union with what the Mahayana Buddhists call "the nature of mind," the Mind that both manifests all reality and is the fundamental consciousness of every human being. As Nyoshul Khenpo Rinpoche writes:

Profound and tranquil, free from complexity,
uncompounded luminous clarity
beyond the mind of conceptual ideas:
This is the depth of the mind of the victorious ones.

In this there is not a thing to be removed,
nor anything to be added
It is merely the immaculate
looking naturally at itself.

Once you experience unity with the One, you understand that all the traditions are describing different faces of the same mystery.

The wisest and most balanced mystical systems all know that the Divine is embodying itself in the universe; they know that, as human beings graced with Divine Consciousness, we are called to unite with the transcendent aspect of the Divine in worship and meditation and with the embodied aspect of the Divine through compassionate action.

The deepest meaning of Sacred Activism, the true source of its power, is that it marries the opposites of the transcendent and immanent divine consciousness and bliss consciousness and peace, with actions of illumined compassion. All the great Sacred Activists know that Divine Love cannot be only an interior experience: after all, it is also the energy that creates and sustains the universe. To live in Divine Love is inevitably to act from it, both by the radiance of your presence and in actual acts of justice and compassion.

What does it mean to live increasingly in a Divine Consciousness that contains both Wisdom and Love and that naturally expresses itself in wise action? It is perfectly expressed by the Isha Upanishad, one of the greatest of all the early Hindu scriptures:

> Who sees all beings in his own Self, and his own Self in all beings, loses all fear. When a sage sees this great Unity and his Self has become all beings, what delusion and what sorrow can ever be near him? The Self filled all with His radiance. He is incorporeal and invulnerable, pure and untouched by evil. He is the supreme seer and thinker, immanent and transcendent. He placed all things in the path of Eternity.
>
> Into deep darkness fall those who follow action. Into deeper darkness fall those who follow knowledge . . .
>
> He who knows both knowledge and action, with action overcomes death and with knowledge reaches immortality.
>
> Into deep darkness fall those who follow the immanent. Into deeper darkness fall those who follow the transcendent . . .
>
> He who knows both the transcendent and the immanent, with the immanent overcomes death and with the transcendent reaches immortality.

It is important that the Isha Upanishad condemns the obsession with Transcendence. The anonymous seer who wrote it had probably himself experienced the depths and dangers of this imbalance—of seeing God only as Absolute Light and not also as every detail of the Creation. The Light has embodied itself as the universe; the true Divine Human knows the transcendent Light in her mind and heart and increasingly in her body and serves its immanent presence in compassionate action toward all beings.

THE THIRD FLAME: THE WORLDWIDE MYSTICAL RENAISSANCE

The third flame of hope that lights up my heart and gives me strength through all challenges is the unprecedented worldwide mystical renaissance that is arising in our time. It is no coincidence that as our desire to exploit and dominate Nature at all costs reaches a climax of destructiveness, a complete, transfiguring mystical awareness explodes from within the human psyche. Anyone who is coming to understand the universe as an incessant dance of opposites will come to see the interconnectedness of these seemingly "opposed" phenomena with a smile of hope.

The unprecedented availability of the world's mystical texts in the world's major languages offers a mélange of paths, any one of which, or any combination of which, can potentially satisfy every different kind of human temperament. If you find the language of Christian mystics too blood-soaked and ecstatic for your taste, you can choose to be initiated into the Sacred through the more sober lucidities of Buddhism. If you find the Buddhist texts too dry and the concept of emptiness as a description of the Divine too impersonal, you can dive into the fire-waters of Hindu devotional mysticism. And if none of these satisfies your particular temperament, you can explore indigenous traditions such as the Hopi or Yamomami; Taoism or Confucianism or the Kabbalah; or the incandescent clarities of Sufism, the mystical core of Islam, the living sap of the great Holy Tree that sprang from the prophet Muhammad's heart. If you don't want to belong to any religious or mystical tradition, you can practice meditation or dedicate yourself to a sacred physical discipline like yoga, Reiki, or Sufi dancing.

There is a downside to this exhilarating variety, of course: you can graze on the different mystical cuisines and never sit down to a serious meal. If you do not have a powerful inner experience, the different names for God and the different "concepts" of the traditions will cause mental confusion rather than spiritual delight. But if you come to this divine smorgasbord with both a humble openness to inner experience and a passion for practice and study, you can make astonishing spiritual progress, and in a way outside the control of the churches and patriarchal guru systems. This allows for the birth of what the contemporary spiritual teacher Caroline Myss calls "mystics without monasteries"—mystics who live their passion for God in the core of life with a radical truth and hunger for social, economic, and political transformation, who need no higher authority than that of the Divine.

It isn't only the revelations and texts of the various mystic traditions that are now widely available; it is also their practices, what the Dalai Lama calls their "technologies of transformation." The texts alone would be inspiring, but to have the practices available to help us realize the deepest meaning of gnosis and revelation at the moment we need them most is a divine grace. Over the last 30 years, practices of every conceivable kind to help transform mind, heart, *and* body have become accessible to any seeker who wants them. This accessibility makes possible, for the first time, the kind of worldwide movement of Sacred Activism that I am hoping for. Every Sacred Activist will be able to realize his or her union with the One in his own way, empowered by his own realization and choice of practices not subject to any controlling human authority. The radical potential of this cannot be overstated.

For me, the single most transforming and hopeful aspect of the mystical renaissance is that it is making a potent and radical vision of the Divine Feminine available to all of humanity. This return to the mother side of God, known and loved in all of the authentic mystical systems, makes the power and consciousness of the Divine Feminine available to us at the moment we need them most. At a time when we are ruining the world and devastating all forms of life including our own, the Mother that creates, evolves, and lives in all things is returning to us to illumine our minds with her knowledge of interconnection, to inflame our hearts with her passion of compassion, and to awaken our bodies by the revelation of her living ecstatic presence. This causes the birth of a humble, exalted, and practical being, a Sacred Activist whose actions inspired by the Mother can potentially transform all the realms of earth life.

Through this potent return of the Divine Feminine and all of its aspects, the Sacred Marriage of Mother and Father, Immanent Godhead and Transcendent Absolute, can now take place within the human race. It is a return to nothing less than the evolutionary power of Divine Love and Wisdom, at work in constant transformation on all the levels of the universe.

As the crisis deepens, the drive to experience this empowering marriage of opposites within us will become more and more insistent and more and more vital to our survival. We are being compelled, through the logic of our own secret destiny, to take a quantum evolutionary leap. This leap could transfigure us and transform all existing social, economic, and political systems so that they honor equality, harmony with nature, justice for all sentient beings, and a sacred way of life that will bring peace to our earth. This is the Hope I have dedicated my life and work to, the Hope that illumines my vision of Sacred Activism.

THE FOURTH FLAME: THE WISDOM OF THE DARK NIGHT

Mystics of many traditions speak of the greatest ordeal of the path as a fierce grace and a miraculous opportunity because it leads to Divine Consciousness. Father Bede revealed this to me out of the depths of his own experience and believed, as I have come to also, that an intimate and unafraid understanding of the Dark Night is the key to the transformation trying to take place in history.

I have experienced in my own life a prolonged and painful Dark Night. I have experienced, too, how knowing what was happening to me and why helped me not only endure it but also be transformed by what I had to live through. When you face this ordeal of transformation, as I believe the world now is, you will not be helped by false optimism or a pseudo-spiritual cheeriness; both will turn to ash in the flames of reality. The only wisdom that will help is the one that knows the flames can, as the alchemists say, "transmute you to burnished gold." The conditions for such a miraculous alchemy are patience, constant spiritual practice, love of God, and complete surrender.

The greatest danger for the world is that as the crisis deepens and the bill for the damage we have done comes due, millions of people will lose faith in themselves and in their version of the Divine, falling prey either to anarchy or to the seductions of authoritarian government. We have already seen what a clever, amoral leadership could accomplish in an America ravaged by fear after 9/11. For eight years, Americans were terrified and unwilling to look at their partial responsibility for what had happened. They allowed the government to lie blatantly, torture the innocent, and instigate an orgy of greed that has devastated the world financial markets, systematically robbing our nation of the very liberties that constituted the essence of American pride, democracy, and freedom. The situation has started to turn around through a growing financial crisis that is awakening millions to the need for change and through President Obama's election; but the damage done to the inner and outer fabric of American life, to America's reputation in the world, and to the all-important cause of environmental change has been drastic. And although everything is now infused with new hope, we would do well to remember what the past years have created, how fragile the human psyche in ordeal is, and what disgraceful things it will do or permit to be done when it feels threatened. This should serve as a permanent wake-up call— and also as a reminder of the new level of spiritual maturity and authentic knowledge we will need if we are to turn the difficulties ahead into opportunities for transformation.

There is a marvelous poem by Rumi in which the mature and authentic wisdom of the Dark Night and its transformation is presented to us in terms of a housewife cooking chickpeas: (one of the many endearing things about Rumi is that he clearly loves to eat—his mystical poetry is full of cooking metaphors.)

The Housewife and the Chickpea

Look at the chickpea in the pot, how it jumps
When it's put into the fire . . .
When you boil the water it's in, the chickpea
Leaps to the top of the pot and cries out,
"Why are you burning me? Wasn't it enough to buy me?
Why do you also have to afflict me?"
The housewife continues to push it down with her spoon,

"Be still and boil well! Don't jump far
From the one who makes the fire!
I don't boil you because I hate you
I boil you to acquire taste and savor
So you can become food and mingle with life:
Your affliction doesn't come from being despised!
When you were fresh and green
You drank water in the garden:
You drank water then to prepare you for this fire."
The mercy of God precedes His affliction.
His Mercy has always preceded His anger
So you can obtain life's authentic wealth.
Chickpeas, you boil in trials and sufferings
So neither self nor existence may remain in you!
Become food, strength, and fine thoughts;
You were weak as milk; become a jungle lion!

I read this poem in terms of the communal Dark Night we are going through. Three essential pieces of life- and sanity-saving information about the rigors of our Dark Night are given here play-fully. First, as the housewife in the poem, the Divine reveals that the Dark Night is not happening because it *hates* humanity, but so that human beings can "acquire taste and savor, become food and mingle with life." In other words, our Dark Night is purifying us and breaking us open so a new emotional depth, tenderness for all life, and sympathy with others can be born.

Secondly, the Divine Housewife reveals that being boiled in the pot in a fierce magical alchemy was prepared through many graces and revelations. As she says to the chickpeas: "When you were fresh and green / You drank water in the garden / You drank water *then* to *prepare* you for this fire" (italics mine). This shows us that coming to our Dark Night is not a curse, but one of the highest and most mysterious of mercies, the condition, in fact, of "obtaining life's authentic wealth."

The third and final reward of this process, the housewife also makes clear, is that where we were "weak as milk" in our selfishness, greed, and dangerous addiction to power of every kind, we now have the chance to be "jungle lions," transformed by suffering, defeat, and destruction into fearless, majestic beings, strong with certainty in our divine identity.

My guide into Rumi was Eva de Vitray-Meyerovitch. I met her in Paris and we became intimate friends who would spend hours talking about our mutual beloved. On her first visit to Rumi's tomb in Konya after 20 years of working with his poetry, Eva met a mysterious old man who gave her a teaching on the meaning and purpose of the Dark Night, which she shared with me. I want to share it with you for its accuracy and beauty:

> I came out into the late afternoon air outside Rumi's tomb and sat down by one of the fountains in the museum's courtyard. I noticed an ancient, wizened Turkish gentleman sitting by my side with a face like a big-eared elf. He was dapper, with brilliant black shoes and a pinstripe suit with a red tie, and smelled heavily of rosewater cologne. Normally I wouldn't have spoken to him. For no reason I can think of, I turned to him and asked him if he knew anything about *fana*, about the Dark Night.
>
> He replied, gazing at me directly, "Through God's grace I have been through it."
>
> I noticed for the first time how beautiful his deep, rich brown eyes were. He took my hand and began to talk quietly and gently as if to his own daughter. This is what he told me:
>
> "To accept that Divine Love will ask us in the end to die into it—that is, for everyone, even the greatest of saints, the hardest of all things on the path. Even Jesus in Gethsemane begged, 'Take this cup from me.' Even Jesus, who had seen God, heard God, healed with the power of God, been seen transfigured by His disciples on Mount Thabor. Even Jesus wept tears of blood at what had to be. So you should not be surprised at rage or fear when you come to your Dark Night. They are natural. They are inevitable. They are part of the process.

"Divine Love begins by seducing you, by kissing you on the inside of your heart. That is how it hooks you. Then it feeds you with ecstasy and vision and revelation, drawing you deeper and deeper into a devouring longing to be one with it. When your longing is great enough and you are surrendered enough to it, Love changes into a Black Lion and tears you limb from limb. Then, when you have been scattered to the four quarters of the universe and not a scrap of 'you' remains and darkness reigns, the Lion turns golden and roars and 'you' are reassembled, resurrected, and your whole being shines with the Glory of the Lion's own Light, the light of the Sun.

"All this is natural and logical in the dimension of Divine Nature and Divine Logic. You cannot begin to understand it through human reason or through the intellect or even through contemplation; you can only begin to understand it through Love. Love itself will teach you what you need. But to be able to learn at all, you will have to have made yourself open through many years of prayer, meditation, and service of all living things and beings."

He smiled and pointed to a rosebush near us with one full, luscious red rose on it.

"The whole meaning of the planting of that bush in the first place was to obtain that open fragrant rose shedding its perfume in all directions. The whole meaning of the Creation is to birth beings like Rumi and Jesus, the full, open, Divine Human roses, who inebriate us all with the fragrance of Divine Passion. Isn't it written in the Koran, 'I was a hidden treasure and I wanted to be known; that is why I created the world'? Those who know the 'hidden treasure' of their innate divinity are those who have opened completely in the Sun of Divine Love. To birth that opening is the secret meaning of the Creation, its goal, its justification.

"Look at that fragrant rose, open so abandonedly, giving itself with such purity and truth to us! Just imagine what has to happen before that bush can produce that rose! First, a clipping must be taken from a healthy original rosebush and planted in good earth; then it must endure living underground and pushing its way upward in the dark; after that, when it finds the sun it has been dreaming of and longing for, it has to protect itself against predators, grow thorns, and struggle to create a solid stem; and after that, it has to fling out from its secret sun-kissed depths such energy and passion that from that stem branches start to grow, branches on which the roses it dreams of making begin, slowly to appear as bigger and bigger buds. All this takes a long time, constant effort, focused passion, season in, season out. Everything has to follow natural order and logic; you cannot go from a clipping to a branch thick with buds directly. All the different stages have to be honored one by one.

"I imagine now that you and I had been sitting here a week ago. What would we have seen where that full rose now is? We would have seen a big, juicy, still-closed bud. What has to happen before the bud can become a rose?"

I was at last beginning to understand. "The Sun has to break it open."

"Yes," he whispered. "The Sun has to train its fire on it and break it open so everything that has been carefully, over many stages, enfolded within the bud can now be unfolded for everyone and so that the perfume the bud is keeping secretly hidden within itself can be given now to everyone who wants it."

His calm voice had spread a carpet of peace over my mind. "You see, my child," he continued, "God as the Sun and the gardener knows what He is doing and what must be done. Yes, this is a terrible alchemy. But it is natural in Divine Nature; the shattering of the bud is the condition of the flaring open of the rose. How can the secret dream of the rosebush and the gardener who planted it be realized if that does not happen?"

We sat silently, and then I said harshly, "What you have told me is fascinating, but there is something too pretty about it all."

My wizened, shining-eyed elf laughed out loud. "Pretty? Have you asked a bud how it feels when it is shattered open? But I know what you mean. Let me try again. All that I can offer you anyway is analogies, images.

"You already know enough," my new friend went on, "to know that fana, or annihilation, the Dark Night, is the ultimate mystery in this life. That is already a blessing. Most people die without even suspecting that there is such a thing as a dying in life that makes you eternal."

"You said you have been through this dying."

"Yes," he laughed gaily like a child. "Yes, thank Allah. And I am only a baby in the new life. Eighty-five years old and a baby. It's silly, but it's true. Blame Rumi! It is all his fault! And now, I'm going to try once again and share with you what Rumi has taught me, and this time I will ask your forgiveness in advance, now that I know how hard you are to enchant.

"Another way of coming to contemplate the mystery of annihilation is to see it as the pangs of a great childbirth. I will explain this slowly." He took my hands in his and patted them tenderly. "Ten years ago, when my time came to be killed by the Lion, I, too, came every day to pray at this tomb and I was lost, angry, and desperate. If you are not lost, angry, and desperate, the Death cannot happen. But there is always protection—you will find this out, perhaps you are finding this out already—and there is always direct guidance for anyone who asks for it. This I know as I know the name of the man who made these black shoes for me. Perhaps the greatest paradox of all the paradoxes that dance around fana is that while you imagine you are at your furthest from God, you are actually so close that you are blinded by His Glory and think it night. Stare into the sun, after all, and your eyes will in the end see only dark; they cannot stand too much Light. What the Darkness really is is the dawning of a Light too immense for your yet-untransformed senses to register.

"But it isn't metaphysical paradoxes that I want to share with you; I want to tell you of what happened to me ten years ago, after I had been praying to Rumi for guidance for a long time. My wife sent me out to buy some bread at about 5:00 one evening. I took the long way round to the baker's, stopping off here at the tomb. I came out, and when I walked out of the front door I saw a young woman lying on the pavement and screaming horrible screams that tore the air and made my blood curdle. I immediately imagined the worst; she must have been raped or stabbed. I ran to her, held her up, and started to look for some telltale wound or bruise. She was too far gone to understand anything I was saying to her, and her screams got worse, and I got more desperate. Suddenly, I noticed that she had spread her legs, and then all of a sudden it struck me: she is screaming because she is giving birth! She wasn't dying at all, she was having a baby! I ran and found an old woman who knew how to deliver children, and the child, a healthy boy, was saved. The woman had been shopping when labor pangs started and had made her way in a hallucination of pain to the entrance of Rumi's tomb, thinking that there she would be safe and find help.

"The screams of the self being torn apart in annihilation, the screams that you hear in Rumi's poetry—all these are not the howls of death but of birth. And Rumi must somewhere have known that; he must have known that what was killing him was also helping him to give birth to the New One in him, the Divine Child.

"Remember what he said in his *Table Talk*:

"This body is like Mary. Every one of us has a Jesus within him, waiting to be born. If pain appears to be our midwife, our Divine Child will be born. If not, our inner Jesus will return to the Origin by the same secret way He came, and we will be deprived of His mystic joy and splendor."

Annihilation, then, is the dark birth canal the inner Jesus has to pass completely through to be born in the Sun. If you can hold to that knowledge and have faith in its reality, through everything, then the Rose of Glory will be opened in you.

I see this dance of destruction and creation happening all around me—the response to eight years of tyranny, inciting the passionate hope that would lead to Obama's election. Without the preceding horror, would America have made the transforming leap to elect an African American president, so opening a new window for hope in the world? I see in my own life and in the lives of my friends how it is heartbreak, defeat, and times of great strife that have not only called forth our greatest resolve, but also birthed our deepest courage, compassion, and creativity. The Hope I am presenting in this book would be far less real if it had not been born out of a prolonged wrestling with all the outer and inner forces that mock at hope.

As Rumi writes:

I have come to a desert where love appears.
My heart is like a vast tablet of light.
An ocean of agony drowned it again and again
But it became a warrior after being martyred a hundred times.
The swells and storms of destiny imperil every ship
But in this sea of Peace all find safety at last.

And, in perhaps his greatest and most comprehensive portrayal of the "wisdom of the dark night" Rumi tell us:

The grapes of my body can only become wine
After the winemaker tramples me.
I surrender my spirit like grapes to his trampling
So my inmost heart can blaze and dance with joy.
Although the grapes go on weeping blood and sobbing,

"I cannot bear any more anguish, any more cruelty!"
The trampler stuffs cotton in his ears: "I am not
working in ignorance.
You can deny me if you want, you have every excuse,
But it is I who am the Master of this Work.
And when through my Passion you reach Perfection,
You will never be done praising my name."

THE FIFTH FLAME: THE SACRED POWER
OF THE DIVINIZED SACRED ACTIVIST

All mystical and shamanic traditions know that as a human
being evolves into union with the One, the One streams powers
to and through her—powers of compassion, of purified passion,
of wisdom, of enhanced creativity, of healing, of energy. We have
already seen in Part I how Jesus in the Gospel of Thomas speaks of
the "finder" of sacred reality coming after an arduous purification
to "reign over everything." Jesus himself exemplified this humble
royalty, displaying the powers given to him by the One in healing after healing, in the intensity and beauty of his presence, in
the healing power and ageless wisdom of his teachings, and in
the greatest miracle of all—that which transmuted the horror of
crucifixion into the glory of resurrection. In living out with such
selfless compassion and passion the powers given to him by the
One, Jesus was showing everyone what could be given to them if
only they could surrender, love, and trust enough.

Jesus makes clear in Logion (saying) 106 of the Gospel of
Thomas that reigning over everything leads to nothing less than a
quantum leap in sacred power: "When you make the two one, you
will become the sons of man, and when you say, 'Monuntain, move
away' it will move away." Jesus is telling us that those who undertake the journey to unify all the opposites within themselves and
so enter into increasingly conscious union with the One become
sons of men. They can tell a mountain to move and it will move.
"Son of Man" is one of the titles given to Jesus himself. It comes

from ancient Jewish prophetic sources and means, in essence, a divinized human being capable of acting as a bridge between the human and divine worlds, imbued with divine power, majesty, wisdom, and transforming love-energy. Jesus is making clear that to those who truly begin to understand the Kingdom within and work with humility to unite the opposites, the One will give a wholly new level of sovereignty. From this level, seemingly miraculous powers—like the ones he demonstrated in healing, exorcising, and walking on water—would flow normally. All ancient and shamanic cultures have always known this great secret.

The ancient wisdom classic I Ching makes explicit this secret knowledge, which is now waiting for all Sacred Activists to reclaim it and be radically instructed and inspired by its truth. In the commentary on Hexagram 16 "Yu" ("enthusiasm"), this miraculous power of sovereignty over reality, of "moving the mountain," is described in a way that is rooted in the customs of ancient Chinese culture but has universal significance:

> In the temple men drew near to God with music and pantomime . . . religious feeling for the Creator of the world was united with the most sacred of human feelings, that of reverence for the ancestors. The ancestors were invited to these divine services as guests of the Ruler of Heaven, and as representatives of humanity in the higher regions. This uniting of the human past with the Divinity in solemn moments of religious inspiration established the bond between God and man. The ruler who revered the Divinity in revering his ancestors became thereby the Son of Heaven, in whom the heavenly and the earthly world met in mystical contact.
>
> These ideas are the final summation of Chinese culture. Confucius has said of the great sacrifice at which these rites were performed that "he who could wholly comprehend this sacrifice could rule the world as though it were spinning on his hand."

The Five Flames of the Sun of Hope

The "Son of Heaven" of the I Ching and the "Son of Man" of Jewish mysticism are different ways of describing the same mystery, that of a human being in union with the One (called in the I Ching the Tao of Heaven and Earth) ruling over the laws of reality with some of the miraculous powers of Divine Grace—ruling the world "as though it were spinning on his hand."

The mystical traditions also warn us—and in the fiercest terms—of what will happen if we abuse the powers that will inevitably come to us on the journey. To use such powers for our own ends and not in pure surrender to the will of the One invites destruction.

The great hope for Sacred Activists is that through understanding the potential for humanity to become instruments of Divine Grace, while heeding the warnings of hubris enshrined in our traditions, we can proceed with great faith and humility to become sons of man and daughters of heaven—empty conduits of a grace and a power that can transform the world.

In one of our private conversations, Father Bede spoke with his characteristic directness, accuracy, and humility about three different stages of this experience of becoming a son of man or daughter of heaven.

"The first stage is what I call the honeymoon stage," Bede said. "This happens at the beginning of the Path when the seeker starts really to fall in love with the Beloved and the Beloved in response sends revelation and profound inner experience. This is a blissful stage that engenders great enthusiasm, faith, passion, delight, and insight, but it is only the beginning. A lot of people find this stage so delightful, exciting, and astonishing that they mistake it for enlightenment.

"If you purify yourself in Stage 1 you will be graced with entry, usually through an experience of Union with the One, into Stage 2. If you are an artist, your art will become transforming; if you are an activist, the energy and passion and wisdom that you will be able to access will astonish and embolden you.

"The great danger at this stage is a subtle one—that you become drunk on the powers that are evolving in you and so, either consciously or unconsciously, misuse them for your own false self.

"If this intoxication with your powers—or rather the powers given to you—becomes permanent, you will either engineer your own destruction or become trapped for decades, or even a lifetime, in what I call 'playing with Light-power.' You will go on using the new powers invested in you to serve your own fame and what you imagine to be 'your mission,' and you will believe your own propaganda about yourself and so be trapped in your subtle ego, which is even more dangerous than being trapped in your ordinary ego.

"No one, in my experience, escapes being burnt by temptation at this second stage. Even Jesus was tempted in the desert after his awakening at the river Jordan.

"I believe that this temptation is in fact essential—because its seduction will show you, as it must have shown Jesus in the desert, just how strong the subtle ego's passion for control, fame, and power remains, even after illumination. And this shadow-knowledge will become your constant and most valuable companion on the path if you always keep turning to it, because it will keep you radically humble whatever happens to you and through you.

"The third stage is what we have talked about—the stage of birthing, of being born yourself into the dimension of the Divine Human through the ordeal of the Dark Night and so becoming a site for the soft explosion of authentic and enormous Divine Grace and Power. No one can become a Birther who has not died to himself or herself, for the simple reason that the Divine *cannot* flow through completely a being who is not completely surrendered."

As Bede was speaking, I remembered a passage I had long loved in the work of Sri Aurobindo that describes precisely what this extraordinary journey requires and what becoming a "Birther" in Stage 3 makes possible:

> While this transformation is being done it is more than ever necessary to keep yourself free from all taint of the

perversions of the ego. Let no demand or insistence creep in to stain the purity of the self-giving and the sacrifice. There must be no attachment to the work or the result, no laying down of conditions, no claim to possess the Power that should possess you, no pride of the instrument, no vanity or arrogance. Nothing in the mind or in the vital or physical parts should be suffered to distort to its own use or seize for its own personal and separate satisfaction the greatness of the forces that are acting through you. Let your faith, your sincerity, your purity of aspiration be absolute and pervasive of all the planes and layers of the being; then every disturbing element and distorting influence will progressively fall away from your nature.

The last stage of this perfection will come when you are completely identified with the Divine Mother and feel yourself to be no longer another and separate being, instrument, servant or worker but truly a child and eternal portion of her consciousness and force. Always she will be in you and you in her; it will be your constant, simple, and natural experience that all your thought and seeing and action, your very breathing or moving come from her and are hers. You will know and see and feel that you are a person and power formed by her out of herself, put out from her for the play and yet always safe in her, being of her being, consciousness of her consciousness, force of her force, Ananda of her Ananda [bliss]. When this condition is entire and her supramental energies can freely move you, then you will be perfect in divine works; knowledge, will, action will become sure, simple, luminous, spontaneous, flawless, an outflow from the Supreme, a divine movement of the Eternal.

When enough Sacred Activists take the journey into becoming sons of man or daughters of heaven, or "Birthers," as Bede put it, or "child[ren] of the Divine Mother," as Sri Aurobindo expresses it, then our actions, born from knowledge, purified will, and Divine

Joy, will become "simple, luminous, spontaneous, fearless . . . a divine movement of the eternal." There is no end to the possibilities for transformation that such a divine movement of Sacred Activists born into this empowered dimension can bring about in the world.

CHAPTER 7

THE DEATH
AND THE BIRTH

We have now arrived at the hardest and most demanding part of our journey together—facing unflinchingly the full extent and real danger of the Death, the Dark Night of the species, that we are living through. No generation has ever had to face so extreme and unprecedented a crisis. All of us, even those of us who have made it our life's work to build in ourselves the faith, courage, hope, and vision to persevere, find it hard.

Even when you know that the Dark Night we are enduring and have to endure is a mystical mystery of Birthing, a complex of dark and disturbing feelings remains, and these feelings need to be worked on and made conscious so they can be transmuted. For those called to be Sacred Activists, this will be a grueling task. There is no magical formula, no quick and neat solution. But there is, I have found, a way through, one that all of us will need to choose and keep choosing as the crisis deepens.

This "way through" is given to us in its highest and most inspiring form by Rumi:

Love's Horse Will Carry You Home

The whole world could be choked with thorns
A Lover's heart will stay a rose garden.
The wheel of heaven could wind to a halt
The world of Lovers will go on turning.
Even if every being grew sad, a Lover's soul
Will still stay fresh, vibrant, light.
Are all the candles out? Hand them to a Lover—
A Lover shoots out a hundred thousand fires.
A Lover may be solitary, but he is never alone:
For companion he has always the hidden Beloved.
The drunkenness of Lovers comes from the soul,
And Love's companion stays hidden in secret.
Love cannot be deceived by a hundred promises;
It knows how innumerable the ploys of seducers are.
Wherever you find a Lover on a bed of pain
You find the Beloved right by his bedside.
Mount the stallion of love and do not fear the path—
Love's stallion knows the way exactly.
With one leap, Love's horse will carry you home
However black with obstacles the way may be.

This is one of the greatest messages ever given to humanity.
Yet for those who are not yet fully grounded in this state of radiant
love and peace, the question remains: how exactly do we acquire
"a lover's heart" that stays "a rose garden" however "choked with
thorns" our circumstances become?

For me, the deepest clue Rumi gives us lies in this couplet:

Wherever you find a lover on a bed of pain
You find the Beloved right by his bedside.

To come to know this and experience it constantly is the great
saving grace and hope of the mystical journey. When you trust
that whatever you have to go through, the Beloved is with you,

showering you with grace and the deepest, most tender compassion, you do not cease to suffer. But instead of being defeated or paralyzed by your suffering, you realize that it has profound meaning, and, slowly, you trust more and more that that meaning will be revealed to you.

As this faith and trust deepen, you find that you can share all the different aspects of your suffering with the Beloved within you and outside you, more and more fearlessly and candidly. As you do so you experience, with ever-deepening wonder, just how all-transforming the Love of the Beloved is, and you come to see that it can give you the humility and strength to transmute even the greatest desperation and anguish.

The consequence of this experience, however, is that you face your own darkest emotions, make them conscious, and offer them up, again and again, for healing and transformation. In the process of uncovering your deepest illusions about your nature, you must embrace your dark inner saboteurs, forgive your resistance to change, and accept, more and more, the heartbreak and unconditional helplessness your ego's strategies have been created to mask and avoid.

This is hard enough to do in an individual Dark Night. When you are also living through a collective Dark Night, it demands even greater faith, trust, and compassion for yourself and others.

What I discovered on my own journey was that I needed to submit myself to two related disciplines to stay hopeful and joyful—a constant discipline of spiritual practice that grounds me in my divine nature and a constant discipline of shadow work that helps me face and transmute the ways in which my personal shadow colludes with the collective shadow cast by our crisis. Spiritual practice, I have found, creates a container strong enough to give me the power to descend into my own anguish and desolation and shadow work, which I have undertaken for several years now with the help of a Jungian analyst, Nathan Schwartz-Salant, who continues to give me deeper and deeper insight into the forces within me and in the culture in general that I need to make conscious in order to offer them up to the Beloved for healing.

The concepts I share with you now are those I have had the privilege of sharing with Sacred Activists all over the world in the course of my teaching. What gives me the greatest hope is that I have found more and more people willing to do the kind of work I am describing, willing to expose their own inner darkness in the trust that making it conscious leads to deeper faith, compassion, and action in the world.

THE FIVE INNER SABOTEURS

I have found five interrelated forms of inner sabotage that are linked directly to the extent of the growing disaster our ignorance, greed, and hubris have engendered.

These "five inner saboteurs" are: disbelief, denial, dread, disillusion, and the desire, in the face of so much danger and heartbreak, to cease to be.

Disbelief

One of the hardest things for any of us to do, I have discovered, is actually to believe we *could* be in such danger. You can understand the danger intellectually and even emotionally, but to accept it with your whole being demands a leap of courage you cannot force but have to prepare for. This is because human beings are conditioned to respond to immediate difficulties but find it hard to respond to a whole cluster of looming disasters for which we have no precedent.

I was talking about this problem with Caroline Myss, who lives around the corner from me in Oak Park. Caroline said, "I have found that it is no use railing at people to wake up; it only increases resistance and doesn't begin to address the real difficulty. This is that none of us have a template for what is happening. All of us have to improvise in the middle of chaos." And then she told me a story: "As you know, I used to live in New Hampshire.

The Death and the Birth

Near where I lived was a quaint little town called Alstead. A few years ago, the entire town, which is in the middle of the country-side, was wiped out by a flash flood created by a cluster of freak circumstances that no one in New Hampshire had any idea could happen. Warning did come in time for the town to evacuate; a sexton started ringing the town bells and shouting over a loud-speaker that a flood was coming. But because no one in Alstead or anywhere else in New Hampshire had any precedent for such an event, no one listened to the warning, the town was wiped out, and several people died."

As she was speaking, I remembered a conversation I had had with a close friend in a fishing village in South India that had been decimated by the tsunami in 2004. He had lost his only son. He told me, "I am a fisherman and pride myself on knowing all the moods of the sea. Nothing in my experience of the sea prepared me for the tsunami. I even saw the wave coming but didn't believe it was what it was, because I had never seen or even imagined a tsunami. I saw my son playing on the beach but didn't even think of catching him up out of harm's way." And then he broke down and sobbed in my arms as I tried to comfort him.

I told the story to Caroline and we both fell silent on her porch, watching the descending summer sun throw longer and longer shadows on her lawn. Then Caroline said, "I think we are all like the villagers of Alstead or your fisherman friend. We all have to face our disbelief at what is happening. Railing at others for not waking up is actually a way of not facing just how many of us still, despite all we know, refuse to acknowledge our situation. If we did *really* acknowledge it, we would all be changing much faster and doing much more."

Her words cut me to the quick, and over the next few days I meditated on what she had said. What I found was that accepting my own continuing disbelief could make me more skillful with the disbelief of others. I used to enjoy railing at others for not *see-ing;* through recognizing my own blindness, I have become more honest and, I hope, more compassionate.

Denial

I used to imagine I was not in denial about what was happening; now I catch myself reeling in and out of denial a hundred times a day, even as I have been writing this book. Sometimes these movements of denial are subtle; sometimes they are so flagrant all I can do is laugh at myself and offer them up to the Divine for illumination. What I am discovering is that thinking you are not in denial is perhaps the most dangerous form of denial in a crisis like ours. It is only by having the courage to unmask the way denial plays out in your innermost thinking that you can begin to be useful.

Dread

Starting to face, without judgment or illusion, my own disbelief and denial has helped me begin to uncover and make conscious the depth of dread I continue to feel. How could any half-conscious human being *not* feel dread at the enormous suffering that is erupting all over the world? Even when you believe, as I do, that this suffering has a meaning and a goal, the extremity of it is overwhelming.

Dread is the most paralyzing of all human emotions and the one I, and everyone else I know, will do almost anything to avoid. Facing the depth of my dread has threatened me, at times, with hopelessness. What I have found, however, is that acknowledging my dread and treating it not as a weakness to be repressed at all costs, but as an inevitable response to real circumstances, has helped me start to heal it. I have found, too, that allowing myself to feel it in my body, in the depths of my gut, has helped me discover that within the body there is what I can only describe as a lake of luminous, spacious peace in which the pain can eventually dissolve.

The Death and the Birth

Disillusion

By facing the inner dread I feel, I have been awakened to the depth of my fourth inner saboteur—a fierce and angry disillusionment with humanity. To experience this disillusionment is to face without denial the reality of the evil that we as a race have done to ourselves, to the animals, and to Nature.

No one who looks unblinkingly at the history of the last hundred years—with their grotesque catalogue of brutal wars, long list of genocides, systematic rape of nature, creation of a free-for-all financial system that makes an elite few obscenely rich while billions of people live in terrible degradation—can avoid seeing that humanity is in danger of losing its conscience and its soul. And no one aware of this can deny to himself that humanity is in terrible shape, at the very moment when it most needs to restore its spirit and rediscover its inner sacred consciousness, not just to repair the inner and outer devastation that has resulted from its actions, but also to survive.

This dark picture is not the whole picture, of course, but it is an essential part of the reason the crisis is unfolding as it is, and it has to be faced without denial. Any vision of hope that glosses over the reality of evil or does not respect its power will not be of any use.

The hardest part of facing your disillusionment with human nature is that it inevitably leads you to disillusionment with your own. We all collude with the system we are in, partly out of necessity but also out of cowardice and a love of comfort. The great majority of us—even those who might have known better—have been seduced by the promises of the corporate propaganda machine of limitless growth and progress.

What I have discovered in my own descent into disillusion is that it is essential to the vision of hope I am offering here. I would not believe in my own vision if it had not weathered the storms of grief and heartbreak and the hopelessness of a long, hard look at our crisis, the state of humanity, and the state of my own character. Although the anguish I felt when I could no longer escape my own inner knowledge did threaten me with despair, its ultimate effect has been to drive me deeper into the truth of my inner Divine Consciousness and to help me finally grasp that our last and best hope is to undergo a transformation that is fierce, inspired, and embodied enough to change the fundamentals of our nature. Sri Aurobindo wrote that "to hope for a true change of human life without a change of human nature is an irrational, unspiritual proposition; it is to ask for something unnatural and unreal, an impossible miracle."

Facing your own corruption and collusion also brings the saving grace of shedding your self-righteousness. Perhaps the greatest enemy to authentic awakening is, as Bede once said, "our utterly unfounded belief in our own spotless virtue." As a spiritual teacher who had a mystical awakening young, my greatest temptation has been to bypass what remains unhealed and dangerous in myself and focus instead on all the revelations I have been given and all the ecstasies I have experienced. Facing my own greed, ambiguity, power hunger, and unconscious addiction to "magical" solutions has, over time, begun to humble me and initiate me into a new-found compassion for others. Like everyone else I know, I have been a fool, blind to my vanities, dressing up my prejudices as "truth," my need to be loved and honored as "selfless service," and my lust for power as my "mission."

When I experienced these failures and derelictions in myself, something extraordinary happened. I felt with an intensity I had never felt before the extravagance of the mercy and forgiveness of God, and I knew, with a clarity that made me break down in wonder, that what I was discovering with shame and great distress, the Divine had always known and always forgiven. I also understood something that brought me to my knees with gratitude—that what had kept me evolving and able to receive grace was not my intelligence or creativity or ability as a teacher, but a love for God so passionate that it carried me through everything in spite of myself, not by my own efforts but through the grace of the Beloved. When you face your own evil, you are rewarded with the knowledge of just how unconditional God's love is and just how miraculously this infinite love will work on the small parts in you that are sincere and devoted, however shaky and compromised they may be, to work its resurrection.

The paradox of such a wonderful and transforming experience is, of course, that it would not have been possible *without* a radical descent into disillusionment. I have had many inner experiences of the love of God, but none that has marked me as deeply as the one I received when at last I was ruined enough by self-recognition to know how absolutely I needed mercy. At the very moment when, through real and inescapable insight into my own darkness, I felt most unworthy of it—and most disturbed about my own future and the future of the world—the Divine Mercy flooded me and revealed to me the ecstatic and tender boundlessness of its infinite love. My deepest hopelessness birthed me into my deepest hope for myself and for everyone else.

The Desire to Cease to Be

There is one more inner saboteur that all Sacred Activists will, I believe, have to face as they try to serve humanity in a time as difficult as ours. This is a desire to cease to be, a desire so intense it almost amounts to a death wish, or, perhaps more accurately, a desire not to have to *feel* anything any more. Emily Dickinson wrote, "After great pain, a formal feeling comes / the Nerves sit ceremonious, like tombs," and every psychologist knows that one of the most distressing and dangerous effects of trauma is the blankness it induces, a kind of death of the spirit.

We are now living in a world in which all of us are consciously or unconsciously traumatized by what we can't help knowing about the world crisis, and this trauma and the desperation it induces fuel a host of addictive behaviors that are driving us into the arms of destruction.

This desire to cease to be or to feel is something I have found in myself and seen in the majority of Sacred Activists I know well. All of us have times when we long not merely for escape or distraction, but for relief from bearing the anguish of lucid compassion and engaged conscience.

What we have to face can kill us. One of my bravest friends, an elderly housewife from the south of France, gave her life to working with indigenous peoples who were threatened by the burning forests in Amazonia. She had an immense gift for friendship and, even in the middle of what she was enduring, would always find time to encourage me with my work. When I think of the support that we as Sacred Activists are going to need it is her face I always see—plump, with ungovernable Einsteinian white hair and glasses she never had the time or money to fix held together with bright red tape.

Last year she committed suicide. She wrote to me and her two other closest friends a letter in which she said, "I have always believed I was so strong, strong enough, with my faith and Provençal peasant genes, to meet any kind of difficulty with my head held high and my heart focused on getting something real and helpful done. I was wrong. The very thing that drove me to do my work—my conscience—has become an unendurable agony to me. In a world descending into barbarism, having a conscience is like having leprosy; it eats you away. Forgive me. I cannot bear the pain of loving the world any more."

I was shocked by her death. She was the last person I could imagine committing suicide. In my arrogance I believed that my mystical awareness would always prevent me from wanting to kill myself.

I was wrong. About three weeks after her death, I spent the morning in a library in New York reading a series of detailed and brilliant articles about the way in which Standard Oil had devastated Nigeria in its drive to control Nigeria's oil. I have spent much of the last five years reading about corporate brutality and environmental devastation in order to arrive at an accurate understanding of what is happening. I began the morning calm and focused, but after two hours of reading about polluted landscapes, ruined rivers, and the deaths of thousands of innocent villagers (while fat-cat CEOs were drinking champagne in Lagos), I began to feel sick to my stomach. I thought I needed some air, so I walked out onto Lexington Avenue.

I stood on the sidewalk, suddenly invaded by the mad noise of the city traffic hurtling past, by the cold horror of what I had been reading. For one blinding moment, all I wanted to do was to step out into the traffic and be run over. It took all the strength I had to restrain myself.

I am grateful for that moment because it helped me share a small part of the pain my friend had felt when she killed herself, and so it filled me with admiration for the heroism that had kept her going so long. I am grateful, too, because that moment forever ended a fiction I had been telling myself about a kind of subtle invulnerability provided by mystical knowledge. Since that moment, I have spoken to many Sacred Activists about the experience; without exception, they have recognized its application to their own lives. When you are "intellectually" concerned about what is happening, you can, at least partially, protect yourself from the pain of the truth; when, however, you decide that you cannot bear to stand by and must do something real, you will inevitably meet the reality of the self-destructiveness that now drives a great deal of human action in the world. If you do not accept that facing this ferocity will bring you to your knees in despair and drive you to wish you had never been born, you will never be able to find the authentic hope that *is* born when you offer up this heartbreak to the Beloved for Him to heal and steady, and so discover that you can bear it without denial and continue to love life.

One of the most transforming paradoxes of the mystical path is that it is our most frightening fragilities that can lead us, if we are humble and lucid enough to work with them, to our most reliable sources of strength. Until I had faced the fact that the work I had chosen to do could drive me to suicide or threaten my sanity, I was in danger from my own unacknowledged shatteredness that I papered over with bravura and rhetoric. Now that I know how demanding authentic Sacred Activism is in a world like ours, I find myself working far harder, both in my spiritual practice and in the analysis I am pursuing with my doctor Nathan Schwartz-Salant, because I know that not only my life's purpose but my life itself depends on them.

I am grateful, too, for the revelation on the sidewalk of Lexington Avenue because it has helped me finally start to take better physical and mental care of myself. One of the great dangers of the "heroic" myth that afflicts and intoxicates many Sacred Activists is that it can lead us—as it has led me again and again—to overestimate our strength and endurance and underestimate the forces of destruction ranged against our truth. This is an extravagance that those of us who believe that the future of humanity now hangs in the balance cannot afford.

THE DEATH AND THE BIRTH

I would like now to present a simple account of the Death and the Birth that are occurring interdependently on the planet. By now it must be clear that I believe that this Death is the birth canal of a new Divine Humanity; that the Birth is already happening; and that Sacred Activism is the force of Divine Love and Wisdom in action, the Birthing Force of the new human.

I shall present the Death first, and as concisely as possible, because in the discussion of the five inner saboteurs I have explored at some length, and as clearly and honestly as I can, what I believe to be the danger and darkness of this Death. Nietzsche writes in *Thus Spake Zarathustra:* "Stare too long into the Abyss and it will stare back into you." I shall keep my account pithy but invite you to let it break your heart open to the anguish and urgency of our situation. Radical heartbreak is, as I will make clear, the thing we all fear most (except death), but is also the condition of finding within ourselves the dedication and passion to midwife the Birth. Rumi writes: "Only the being whose robe is torn by great heartbreak will be given the purity and power of Divine Love." He also writes: "In the broken-open heart you will find a fountain of deathless passion that will never run dry."

In my vision of them, the Death and the Birth each have seven main aspects that, as you will see and experience, are interlinked.

The Death

1. Environmental devastation. The environmental holocaust is progressing faster than the most pessimistic doomsayers a decade ago predicted. One hundred and twenty species disappear into extinction every day. If current rates of unregulated devastation continue, the Amazonian rain forest, the lungs of the world, will be gone by 2050. All of the world's seas are horribly polluted. Both poles, as well as the glaciers of Greenland, are melting at a much more rapid rate than scientists once thought, with the prospect of a rise in sea levels that could displace and claim the lives of 100 million people within 50 years; the melting of the glaciers in the Himalayas, numbering almost 50,000, is set to force water shortages across Southeast Asia, since many of the area's largest rivers—the Indus, Ganges, Yellow, and Yangtze rivers, for example—are fed by the Himalayan ice fields.

This is just a tiny glimpse of the devastation taking place. Extensive and accurate information is now easily available on all aspects of the crisis. But little is being done on a global scale to deal with such a huge and unprecedented situation, a situation that Kofi Annan, then secretary-general of the United Nations, characterized soberly in an article he wrote for *The Washington Post* in November 2006: "Climate change has profound implications for virtually all aspects of human well-being, from jobs and health to food security and peace within and among nations. Yet, too often, climate change is seen as an 'environmental problem' when it should be part of the broader development and economic agenda. Until we acknowledge the all-encompassing nature of the threat, our response will fall short." It is still falling short, absurdly short, and time is running out.

2. Population explosion. Demographers predict that the current population will triple to nine billion by 2050—at least three billion people more than the planet can support, according to many scientists. Peter Wadhams, professor of ocean physics at the University of Cambridge, wrote in his introduction to

Catherine von Ruhland's *Living with the Planet* (Lion, 2009), "An uncontrolled population explosion must lead to mass starvation since the increased agricultural productivity of the planet is coming up against the constraints of limited land, diminishing water resources, and loss of farmland to biofuel production. Yet there is no sign that the lesson of overpopulation, learned in the 1960s, is being remembered. Similarly, the gigantic industrialization effort underway in China and India, as well as being a major source of greenhouse gases, is destined to fail since there are simply not enough resources in the form of oil, coal, and minerals to support industrial powers with such huge populations."

This out-of-control population explosion means that savage wars are likely to be fought in the near future over the simplest and most essential items—food and water. Ismail Serageldin, then vice president of the World Bank, said in 1995 that "the wars of the next century will be about water."

Population explosion also means that the already vast gap between the rich and the billions of poor is widening more all the time. Anyone who has been to the slums of Mumbai or Manila or Phnom Penh or Nairobi will know what this means: hundreds of millions of people all over the world are living lives of helpless degradation in filthy cramped quarters with no money, no medical supplies, and no hope for a better way of life. This terrifying poverty—in which two billion people live on less than a dollar a day—is an ideal breeding ground for terrorism, and anarchic violence.

3. The growth of fundamentalism and religion-inspired terrorism. Rather than coming together and relinquishing their mystically illiterate claims to exclusivity, a large part of the world's religions are retreating into violent separatism, when the world needs to be united more than ever. This amounts to a destruction of our inner world as great as the devastation wrought by free-market fundamentalism on our outer world. We have already experienced this danger in the disaster of 9/11, and in the even greater disaster of the Bush administration's response in Iraq and Afghanistan.

The danger becomes more ominous when you realize that all the religions of the Bible—Christianity, Islam, and Judaism—contain growing fundamentalist sects that envision Armageddon scenarios centered on Israel. This shared obsession could turn what is already the most volatile political situation on earth into a war fought by world powers, all supposedly with God on their side. Such a war could end life on earth. It would represent the ultimate demonic parody of the authentic Divine and its all-embracing Love of all beings.

4. Nuclear proliferation. The destructive passions within the human psyche have always been able to cause chaos and suffering, often on a considerable scale. But while these destructive passions may not have changed over the course of our history, the powers at their disposal have made a quantum leap with the development of the nuclear and hydrogen bombs in the last two decades. The fall of Soviet Russia, the rise of Islamic terrorism, and the proliferation of nuclear, biological, and other weaponry has further destabilized the situation. Even the most sober political experts I know speak of the near-certainty of a nuclear terrorist explosion occurring within the next ten years in a European or American city, unless a major transformation takes place in the relationship between the West and the terrorist wing of Islam. With India and Pakistan, both now armed with nuclear weapons, teetering on the edge of war in the wake of the Mumbai terrorist incident, and with China's nuclear ambitions on the world stage murky at best and the Middle East in the grip of its most brutal crisis in 40 years, the odds of avoiding large-scale nuclear war are shrinking exponentially.

5. Our technological worldview. We have turned the earth into a great cement garden, causing incalculable damage to both our outer and our inner world through our desire to exploit and dominate nature with technology, our fantasy about the limitless powers of scientific progress, and our deranged obsession with limitless growth. To feed our addiction, we have had to destroy all vestiges of our sacred relationship with Nature. The sense of meaninglessness and desolation this has ingrained in us makes us even more prone to destroy the Nature we no longer care about. A New Yorker friend of mine said recently, "The nearest I and most of my friends ever get to Nature is a salad. How do you expect us to *care* about it?" We have turned our addictive celebration of the powers of science and technology into a war against Nature that can only end in self-destruction, unless we transform our relationship with both the authentic Divine and Nature itself—the two interrelated fountains of radiant beauty and energy that work to restore and refresh us.

6. The corporate mindset and the corporate-controlled media. Everyone knows that the world is largely run by multinational corporations with no legal accountability that bribe and corrupt governments, pursue policies of naked greed, and control most of the political parties and institutions all over the world that could restrain their power. The world economy is headed toward an unprecedented global recession, and the limitless greed of the corporate mindset, its sanctification of the bottom-line mentality, is matched only by its limitless folly and capacity to believe its own propaganda. There is a terrible humor in all this, and as everyone also knows in a further dark twist of the joke, it is not the rich, but the poor who are paying the price for the madness of the financial markets.

To make an already bad situation worse, a handful of rightwing corporations largely controls the media as well as everything else. At a time when the world needs to be informed about the true dimensions of the crisis we are living through and requires every available form of encouragement and inspiration, it is kept instead in what I call a "Coca-Coma," stupefied by celebrity trivia, halfbaked news, and a 24-hour diet of inane comedy shows, advertisements, pornography, and violence that keep us docile and infantile, addicted to the consumerism that is killing us even as it feeds our already dangerous levels of alienation and fear. We have become so used to this incessant, systematic psychic rape that we hardly notice it anymore; the anomie of the abused has become a normal state of mind.

7. Our hectic pace of life. This is perhaps the single most dangerous aspect of our contemporary mindset, and one that is invaluable to those powers that want to keep us obedient and unempowered. If you believe, as I do, that the hope for our survival lies in a massive spiritual transformation that expresses itself in radical action, then you observe the driven and hysterical pace of life in our times, and shudder at our institutionalized (even celebrated) universal ADD that deprives us of the one thing we now need most—some quiet leisure in which we can connect with the Divine in Nature and within us.

The authentic mystical transformation is hard to accomplish in such a whirlwind of empty striving and meaningless hyperactivity. It is hard for people to choose a life dedicated to Sacred Action when they have a family to feed and a status to maintain.

When you are brave enough to allow yourself to experience all seven aspects of the Death simultaneously, the only sane, human, and useful reaction is heartbreak. This, of course, is the reaction we all fear most, because we are all afraid that actually waking up to what is really happening will either kill us or drive us mad. But the truth the mystical systems tell us—one we deeply need to hear—is that if we can create a container of trust strong enough, this necessary heartbreak will not only *not* destroy us; it will open us to unprecedented graces of energy and transformation.

I am writing this book with the energy, hope, and passion that only my experiences with repeated heartbreak could have given me. I have learned in the core of my being what Rumi meant when he wrote, "In the ruin of heartbreak, you find the diamond of a divine passion that can resurrect the dead."

What I have discovered for and in myself is that allowing yourself to experience the kind of cosmic heartbreak I am describing, as long as you are grounded in spiritual practice and trust in God, leads not to death but to a far more abundant life; not to madness that annihilates, but to the madness that creates and keeps loving, working, hoping through everything—the sober madness of an unconditional, ever-increasing compassion in action.

The reason I stress the "sacred" in Sacred Activism is that I know from my own deepest experience that if you do not understand such massive heartbreak as a necessary stage of initiation into the extremity and saving madness of Divine Love, there is great danger in approaching it. With mystical knowledge and practice, you are strong enough to accept the shattering by heartbreak and the rekindling in its fires of your whole being and life's purpose. Without mystical knowledge and practice, it would be hard not to be ruled by fear and dominated by the prevailing culture of detachment, which will only keep you from your own deepest sources of compassion and joy, passion, purpose, and hope. The future hope of Sacred Activism rests with beings who are courageous, loving, and grounded enough in sacred knowledge and mystical peace to endure the heartbreak of experiencing the Death as it really is, and so to experience the Birth into a new state of empowerment with urgent passion and compassion and wisdom. During the last few years, I have met thousands of people who allowed themselves to be dragged through their own Dark Nights into a deeper and wilder love for all beings. I know that what the vision of Sacred Activism demands is difficult and sometimes scary, but with grace, humility, and work, it is far from impossible.

Rumi wrote:

There is no salvation for the love
But to fall in love.
Only lovers can escape
Out of these two worlds
This was ordained in creation.
Only from the heart
Can you reach the sky
The rose of glory
Grows from the heart.

For the Rose of Glory to start growing from the heart, the heart has to let itself be broken open. As Rumi writes:

The Death and the Birth

> When the agony of love has broken open your life
> Roses and lilacs take over the garden of your soul.

When "roses and lilacs take over the garden of your soul," a transforming power of sacred passion is birthed in its core.

And, as Rumi tells us in one of his greatest poems that celebrates the transforming potency of this passion:

> Passion burns down every branch of exhaustion;
> Passion is the Supreme Elixir and renews all things;
> So don't sigh heavily, your brow bleak with denial,
> Dare to look for Passion, Passion, Passion, Passion! . . .
> Futile solutions deceive the force of passion,
> They are bandits who extort money through lies! . . .
> Run far away, my friends, from all false solutions!
> Let Divine Passion triumph and rebirth you in yourself!

Letting your heart break open, then, leads to the triumph of rebirth in your true self, the Divine Self that loves all beings with a passion of compassion and works tirelessly and joyfully to serve and help others.

The Birth

Let us turn now to the Birth, the Birth of a new Divine Humanity that is taking place as a passionate response to the Death that millions of us are now waking up to. The necessity of a new way of being and doing everything is proven by Obama's historic victory, which would have been impossible without a grassroots movement that embraced many different kinds of people—black, white, young, old, Democrat, and centrist Republican—who might disagree, for example, on religion or gay rights, but who know that the old way of market fundamentalism, exploitation of Nature, governmental secrecy, and imperialist ambition is now literally and metaphorically bankrupt. This constituency—which Paul Ray calls "cultural creatives"—has been slowly arising since the '60s. Now, in President Obama, in the team he has assembled with him, and in the policies he is trying to implement, we see that the time has come for the "cultural creatives" to put into practice the vision of justice, equality, and harmony with nature that has been inspiring them and giving them purpose through the long Dark Night of the last decade. This is a momentous time, fraught with danger, but the fact that it is here shows anyone who has been waiting for the Birth that its existence no longer has to be asserted; it is in plain view.

Here are what I consider to be the seven most important features of this Birth.

1. The crisis itself and the response to it. By now you know that I consider the intensity and force of the Death we are going through a blessing, because it is a wake-up call that no one will be able to ignore. It is a blessing also because it is awakening, on a massive scale, a response of creativity and selfless service among those who recognize what a crucial time it is and see that anything is now possible—the best as well as the worst.

The most hopeful expression of this new wave of extraordinary creativity and desire to serve has been, I think, definitively identified by Paul Hawken in his book *Blessed Unrest.* Inspired by a growing sense of urgency and the discovery that his feelings of radical distress were shared by thousands of like-minded people who were actually trying to enact change, Paul Hawken set out to find out just how many progressive movements—movements devoted to causes such as the environment, human rights, gay and lesbian rights, animal rights, and so on—had been sparked by the growing disaster. His discovery filled him with hope; he calculated that there are between one and two million organizations on the earth now actively working toward ecological sustainability and social justice.

Such a movement, on such a scale, has never before been seen. Just as the Death we are living through is on a global scale, so is the answering response of creativity and sacred service. For those who can see the global scale, intensity, passion, and inventiveness of this response, it is the Sign that the Birth is now happening everywhere. It is important to see this clearly, but not to become triumphant or smug; the forces ranged against this Birth still have enormous power, and the "movement" itself is still far from being organized or coherent. The future depends not only on the skill of President Obama and his team, but on the way in which all of us who hope so profoundly for his policies to succeed now go beyond whatever differences we have and join together to help in the rebirth. This is why I believe the vision of Sacred Activism I am presenting is important; it challenges us to go beyond our habits of consumerism, apathy, and dissociation and to meet, with resolve and hope, the great historical opportunity that has manifested.

Paul Hawken describes this disparate movement of concerned activists of every stripe in this way: "It claims no special powers and arises in small discrete ways, like blades of grass after a rain. The movement grows and spreads in every city and country, and involves virtually every tribe, culture, language, and religion, from Mongolians to Uzbeks to Tamils. It is composed of families in India, students in Australia, farmers in France, the landless in Brazil, the Bananeras of Honduras, the 'poors' of Durban, villagers in Irian Jaya, indigenous tribes of Bolivia, and housewives in Japan. Its leaders are farmers, zoologists, shoemakers, and poets." Paul Hawkins describes this movement as having three fundamental and interconnected branches: one of social justice issues, one of environmental activism, and one of the fight of indigenous peoples against corporate domination.

It is the genius of Paul Hawken in *Blessed Unrest,* and of Paul Ray's meticulously researched vision of the cultural creatives, that this "movement" of already active people—who represent, as Hawken says so rightly, the majority of human beings alarmed about the future—is now clearly identified for anyone to see, draw hope and inspiration from, and join with.

One of my prayers for Sacred Activism is that it will provide the inspiration and tools for this "movement" to at once be grounded in mystical reality, with all the hope and sacred power that that can provide, and more coherently interlinked and organized. But the "movement" is here; you and I are part of it.

2. Creative technologies. When you begin to grasp just how interconnected the Death and Birth are, you also start to see how the darkest "powers" of the Death are constellating new and forward-looking responses. New discoveries and possibilities are being opened up in every realm of science—from astrophysics to genetic and stem-cell research—and in the various branches of technology. If we have the political and spiritual will to use them wisely, they will transform our world.

The best example is in a wholly new range of energy sources that have been developed. These include ethanol and biofuel, solar and wind energy, energy drawn from algae and sea tides, hydrogen energy, and more. While no one believes that our addiction to oil will relinquish its hold immediately, in spite of the obvious harm it is doing, the fact remains that there is an extraordinary array of real and potent possibilities for new energy currently available. What is more, they are ready to be used on a large scale, if the political and social will to do so arises.

I am convinced that this social and political will *will* arise. The millions who elected President Obama *want* a new energy policy, and President Obama has the political mandate and the team to bring one in. Besides, the inevitable environmental disasters ahead will wake up even those who have remained asleep. We are in a race against time, but the signs show that more and more people all over the world understand that we must restructure society around sustainable energy if the world is to survive. People everywhere are starting to be willing to make the necessary sacrifices for a new way of life.

3. New forms of democratizing media. *I* have been extremely critical of the media's emphasis on celebrities, violence, pornography, and inane reality shows at a time when everything truly important is at stake. But over the last ten years there have been signs that even in Hollywood, a new kind of serious responsibility toward world issues is emerging. Look at the later work of George Clooney, for example. *Syriana* and *Michael Clayton* are both brilliant and searing explorations of problems central to our time. Look at the work Anderson Cooper has been doing with such dry wit and sophisticated ferocity on CNN: the series "Planet in Peril" explored some of the most drastic aspects of our crisis and exemplified what serious reporting coupled with well-chosen, powerful imagery can yield. Look, too, at the hilarious, devastating (and extremely successful) documentaries of Michael Moore and the worldwide reach of Al Gore's brave and clear *An Inconvenient Truth,* which awakened millions to the reality of environmental devastation.

The most empowering and hopeful development in media, however, is the explosion of the Internet. In the very moment when the world is threatened by the kind of tribal and religious divisiveness I described as part of the Death, we find a wholly democratic tool for connecting people that extends beyond the reach of governments, organized religions, or corporations. Nothing illustrates its potential better than President Obama's victory, which was due in large part to his team's invention of a new and daring grassroots Internet organization. Obama will, I am certain, continue to refine this organization and utilize the Internet in new and startling ways to connect people and disseminate crucial information.

In the years to come, the Internet will provide an effective way of coordinating grassroots protests against the war machine, polluting corporations, and fascist entities, as well as flexible, responsive ways of organizing the "movement" that Paul Hawken and Paul Ray describe.

Few things are more important for the future of the Birth than keeping the Internet truly open and free from governmental and corporate pressures to control it. When Yahoo! acceded to the Chinese government's demand that access be controlled in China, it set a disgraceful and dangerous precedent. With so much at stake, the powers that be will do everything they can to manipulate, censor, or shut down the Internet. Sacred Activists must see to it that these efforts are exposed and resisted.

4. The mystical renaissance. At a time when the fundamentalism in most of the world's traditions is wreaking greater and greater havoc, a potent antidote to its madness is arising in the form of a worldwide mystical renaissance. I have written at some length about this; here, I want to remind you of the three most empowering aspects of this renaissance, the three that are helping to engender the Birth.

The first is that all the major texts of all the world's religions are now accessible to anyone who wants to read them. This accessibility—coupled with the fact that all of the world's major mystical traditions are still intact, available for seekers to explore and engage with—means that anyone who wants to can now take the journey to the Divine in terms of his or her own temperament and personal inclination. This amounts to a revolution of personal mystical freedom.

The second empowering aspect of this renaissance—and the clue to its potential effectiveness in Sacred Activism—is the fact that along with the texts and traditions of the mystical traditions, their practices, their "sacred technology of transformation," are now available as well. Traditionally, such practices were kept confined within the walls of monasteries; now they are accessible to anyone who wants to work with them humbly and seriously. This amounts not only to a revolution of personal mystical freedom, but also to a revolution of personal mystical *transformation* and radical empowerment. Sacred Activism as I am envisioning it would be impossible without this revolution.

The third aspect of this renaissance that is crucial to the Birth is the fact that it is starting to make available—to those who want it—the kind of radical evolutionary mysticism that has inspired this book. The Birth, as I have experienced and tried to describe it, is a Birth of the Divine in the heart of matter, a birth of the Divine in the human; the return of the Mother, of the Divine Feminine in all her forms and powers—nourishing and devastating, peaceful and outraged—makes possible for the first time in human history on a large scale a radical embodied mysticism that could help us imagine and implement a new future.

What this embodied evolutionary mysticism makes possible is the kind of evolutionary leap that hundreds of thousands of people will need to take for the world to be not only preserved, but renewed and transformed. I am convinced that hundreds of thousands *will* take this leap. The embodied mystical vision of radical transformation of self and world that has appeared in the work of Teilhard de Chardin, Sri Aurobindo, Father Bede Griffiths, and Ken Wilber—and in this book—shows me that the Birth will be embraced and implemented by all those whom the Divine is awakening. In the epoch of humanity's most self-destructive self-betrayal, the greatest, richest, and most transforming vision of its potential has arisen to give it hope and to guide it forward.

5. The evolving philosophy of nonviolence. The 20th century was the bloodiest century in humanity's history. In 2009, our world stands poised on the brink of many violent crises, each of which has the potential to cause great calamity. Yet in the middle of this violent century, and partly as a response to its violence, a path of nonviolent resistance emerged.

Through this path of nonviolent resistance, Gandhi was eventually able to end British imperialism in India; through it, Martin Luther King, Jr., was able to transmute the justifiable outrage of African Americans after two centuries of oppression into a commitment to hold the high moral ground of justice and forgiveness; through it, Lech Walesa was able to engineer the victory of the Solidarity movement in Poland, triggering the chain of events that led to the collapse of the Soviet empire; through it, Nelson Mandela and Bishop Desmond Tutu were able to bring an end to apartheid and ensure that the transition to a new society in South Africa would be done in the spirit of reconciliation and forgiveness, not hatred and civil war. Through his unwavering commitment to this path, the Dalai Lama has been able to save Tibetan spiritual culture, if not Tibet itself, and so spread its wisdom throughout the world when it is needed most.

These achievements in the face of brutal opposition show that when human beings are grounded in the sacred depths of their nature and act with compassionate intention and resolve, divine blessing descends on their actions and ensures that, in time, what they are struggling to achieve can be achieved.

In other words, when human beings act according to the deepest sacred truth of respect and compassion for others, the Divine protects and furthers what they are attempting to achieve. This great and holy law is known throughout all the mystical traditions and is nowhere better expressed than in the I Ching, in the commentary on Hexagram 25, Wu Wang, "innocence":

> Man has received from heaven a nature innately good, to guide him in all his movements. By devotion to this divine spirit within himself, he attains an unsullied innocence that leads him to do right with instinctive sureness and without any ulterior thought of reward and personal advantage. This instinctive certainty brings about supreme success and "furthers through perseverance" . . . Confucius says about this: "He who departs from innocence, what does he come to? Heaven's will and blessing do not go with his deeds."

As a race, we have begun to believe that the only way to achieve anything is through the use of force. This is the most dangerous of illusions, as wars and genocides prove. The efforts of the quiet heroes of passive resistance I have already cited, as well as many others—Rosa Parks, Cesar Chavez, Rigoberta Menchu— are the one way out of this lethal delusion.

I am not a dogmatic pacifist, however. In certain extreme situations—which I pray do not arise, but could—I would be prepared to take up arms and use force. Sri Aurobindo was right to attack Mahatma Gandhi for his belief that the Nazis could be stopped by nonviolent protest; in fact, Gandhi's peaceful and luminous nature drastically underestimated the extent of the Nazis' embrace of evil. Sri Aurobindo knew that humanity had reached a point where its future evolution was in extreme danger and that if the Nazi threat was not met with victorious force, the unfolding of the Divine in the human would be destroyed.

It is possible that we may soon come to such a moment again. When we do, if we wish to preserve the possibility of the Divine Adventure, we will have to use force. When I spoke to the Dalai Lama in 1989, he agreed, making it clear that he is not a dogmatic pacifist either. He said to me: "In certain very rare, extreme cases, force may be necessary." Then he added: "But the only people who could be hoped to use such force economically and with compassion would be those who had undergone a long spiritual discipline and a long training in nonviolent resistance."

What His Holiness said had the unmistakable ring of difficult and complex truth, and I think it offers a way forward for Sacred Activists that is rooted in the "innocence" the I Ching celebrates but also gives a signal to the powers that be that Sacred Activists are a power to be reckoned with. At the same time, our commitment to use passive nonviolent resistance wherever possible sends the message that we strive for a harmonious resolution and will work tirelessly for it. President Obama expressed this marriage of opposites perfectly in his inauguration speech when he said, "To those who cling to power through corruption and deceit and the silencing of dissent, know that you are on the wrong side of history, but that we will extend a hand to you if you are willing to unclench your fist."

Such a position may be more difficult to hold than either that which condones reactive violence or that which maintains only nonviolent resistance, but we must be willing to try. While I believe in what the I Ching says about "unsullied innocence" and the blessing it brings down on our actions, I also know that there is a fierce side to the Divine, which can on rare occasions destroy in order to protect the truth. The Sacred Activist will need to be so surrendered to the will of the Divine so that he or she will know what to do when circumstances arise, and stay surrendered so as to be guided in *how* to do it.

6. The return of the Divine Feminine. A feminine understanding of interconnectedness and sacred equality and harmony is seeping into all areas of our lives to open us to its transforming truth. Here, I want to invite you to see how this is happening.

In a sense, all of the first five aspects of the Birth we have discussed can be seen as radiating from this potent return of the Divine Feminine. The movement I described in the first aspect is dedicated to protecting life against our prevailing culture of death. It is the Light of the Mother that is illuminating the minds of scientists everywhere and helping birth the new technologies that will preserve the earth; the amazing visions that physics opens up of interrelatedness on every level of the universe mirror what the mystical traditions have long understood about the Mother-Force of God; as ecology develops, it celebrates with greater and more revealing detail just how all-embracing this interrelatedness is and how our survival now depends on honoring it and reinventing our way of life to reflect it.

I have pointed out that the existence of the Internet enables new and revolutionary possibilities for the dissemination of information and the interlinking of movements of dissent and protest. The path of nonviolent resistance, with the use of force in rare, extreme circumstances that I propose in aspect 5, incarnates everything I have come to learn about the Mother's own divine nature. She will work for harmonious resolution, but in extreme circumstances, when it is necessary, she will destroy in order to protect creation from destruction.

In the last three decades, this vision of the Divine Feminine has begun to permeate and elevate our understanding. I see this in ten important areas: in the influence of holistic medicines that honor the interconnectedness of mind and body; in the evolution in the business world of models of interaction that stress cooperation, mutual respect, and creativity rather than competition; in the leap we have made in our recognition of the sacredness and rights of animals; in the expansion of women's rights, despite the violent efforts of fundamentalists everywhere to oppose them; in the progress of gay rights; in the evolution of a radical new vision of the Sacred Masculine that does not effeminize masculinity, but defines its strength and nobility as its capacity to revere, protect, and integrate the feminine; in the expansion of sacred physical disciplines such as yoga and Reiki, which help those who practice them enter into the sacred joy of embodiment; in the proliferation of forms of therapy that, like the Jungian, honor the sacredness of the shadow and the body; and in the growth in many areas of science—physics, ecology, neurobiology—of our knowledge of interdependence.

This return of the force of the authentic Divine Feminine conveys to us, for the first time in human history, on a grand scale and with real potential for transformation, what we might call the Wisdom of the Sacred Marriage—a wisdom that fuses all opposites, "masculine" and "feminine," scientific and mystical knowledge, technological and spiritual power—within a vision of Sacred Activism that can not only help preserve the world, but birth a new Divine Humanity. It is perhaps because of this—because they see this Wisdom-and-Love-in-Action beginning to manifest with great power on the earth—that the forces of domination and exploitation are wreaking such havoc everywhere. It is as if they know that their days may be numbered, that a new vision of Divine Force is coming to transfigure the terms and conditions of life on earth, and so they will do anything—even risk the extinction of the earth itself—rather than lose their hold.

The very desperation of this reaction shows that these forces know they have lost already. If they destroy the world, they destroy themselves, and if they continue to rage with such undisguised and brutal intensity, they are bound to provoke opposing and overwhelming reactions that will, in the end, dissolve their power. This is the final paradox of history, in which the Divine will have the last word, as it had the first.

7. The Divine willing and blessing the Birth of the Divine Human. The Divine I know is at once utterly transcendent and immanent in every flea and stone, at once Father and Mother, at once perpetually free of the turmoil of history and involved in every aspect of it. No language has ever been able to express such a paradox, but through Divine Grace it is possible to experience it.

Once this One Consciousness that is both transcendent and immanent, "passive" and "active," utterly still and always evolving, has been experienced, it becomes clear that the destiny of humanity and the true meaning of history is to give birth to this consciousness on earth so that all conditions and all living matter on earth can be transformed.

This Birth is now taking place. The Divine is blessing it, making it possible, and pouring down torrents of grace to water, nourish, sustain, and inspire it. The crisis we are going through is itself an aspect of this blessing; it is the most powerful sign imaginable that the Light propelling this evolution is simultaneously exposing every illusion and turning an unwavering beam on every lethal shadow, making one choice ever clearer for the human race—change or die.

Someone who chooses the transformation of radical embodiment and Sacred Activism will not have an easy life or guaranteed success. What she will have is the certainty of being on a supreme Sacred Adventure. What she will receive for all she gives and endures is the increasing love and wisdom consciousness of the One, in a body, on the earth. What she will increasingly become is a conscious instrument of the Will that wills the Birth. What she will live in is hope that no defeat can destroy: what she will know is the peace and joy that death itself cannot annihilate. As Rumi writes:

> Such a person does not define his life for himself
> Nor does he hanker after the glory of a life to come:
> For him, living and dying are the same thing.
> He lives for the love of God: he dies for the love of God
> And not out of any fear or any suffering.
> He does not hunger for the trees and rivers of paradise.
> His faith is perfect in his passion to do God's will.

The reward of such a faith and surrendered passion is nothing less than to live, while in a body, something of the divine life on earth.

CHAPTER 8

THE FIVE FORMS
OF SERVICE

I have tried to give you as rich and potent a vision of the Birth as I could. But visions, however inspiring, cannot transform the difficult realities of the world unless they are grounded in a daily routine.

So how exactly do you become a midwife of the Birth in the heart of ordinary life? I believe that it is by making a steady commitment to combine five interlinked forms of service—service to the Divine, service to yourself as an instrument of the Divine, service to all sentient beings in your life, service to your local community, and service to the global community.

Think of these five forms of service as the five fingers of your hand stretched out to bless and help the world.

SERVICE TO THE DIVINE

Without constant divine help, grace, illumination, and strength, no one can be a Sacred Activist, especially in a world as challenging as ours. So turn to the Divine in whatever way you imagine it and serve it in devotion and adoration and gratitude and praise, asking it constantly and humbly to illumine your mind with sacred wisdom, keep your heart on fire with a passion of compassion for all beings, and keep filling your body with sacred energy for whatever work it calls you to do in the world.

SERVICE TO YOURSELF AS AN INSTRUMENT OF THE DIVINE

A Sacred Activist wants to be as healthy and strong as possible to do the work. The Birth of the Divine in the body and in the world through Sacred Activism requires that we look after ourselves seriously.

One of the great lessons that loving the Divine Feminine has begun to teach me is how to mother myself, how to make sure that the instrument I am using to try to do Her will in the world is treated with something of the Mother's tenderness and respect. This means looking after the soul through sacred practice, looking after the mind through constant inspiration, looking after the heart and its emotions by deep shadow work, and looking after the body by diet, exercise, and sufficient rest.

For most Sacred Activists the greatest challenge is look after the body. Many of us have inherited a belief that the body is inferior, something we have to compel to do the will of our heart and spirit. This is a great mistake. How can the Birth take place in the body if we do not revere and cherish it? And how can we keep working with sacred energy and balance in the world if our bodies are under assault from our own body shame and our own careless habits? Try to eliminate everything in your life that compromises your body's health—poor eating habits, stressful situations, lack of sleep. You will find that being a mother to yourself in this way will bring a peace and joy into your life that acts as a perfect "ground" to receive the Divine Energy.

Father Bede once said to me, "Imagine that God is a great musician and that you are a flute He wants to play the most glorious music on. If the stops of your flute are filled with mud, how can the music that is meant to be played through you sound at all?" By removing the mud from the "stops" of your sacred instrument—yourself—with prayer, inspiration, and diet, exercise, and rest, you can allow your body to renew itself and live in balance.

There is nothing narcissistic about this care you give yourself to stay as clear and balanced an instrument for the Divine as possible. Every human being is an incarnation of the Divine waiting to discover the truth of his or her real identity; by honoring and taking care of all aspects of your human self, you are honoring your creator, whose presence in you is your secret truth. Your human self is the living temple of your Divine Self; doesn't your Divine Self deserve its temple to be as strong and balanced as possible?

If you honor the need to serve yourself as an instrument of the Divine, you will discover, over time, that you will have far more compassionate and healthy energy to give to your work in the world. You will also find that because you are truly treating yourself with patience, generosity, and respect, you naturally treat others better; how we treat ourselves is mirrored in the way we treat others.

Because I have always found this sacred service of myself hard to do and have had to remind myself constantly of its necessity, I have written a short prayer that I will share with you:

Divine Mother, give me Your eyes so I can see myself through them and see how holy in Your eyes is my soul, and how holy in Your eyes is my mind, and how holy in Your eyes is my heart, and how holy and sacred in Your eyes is my body. Help me be as merciful and generous with myself as You would always want me to be; help me honor myself as I have found to my amazement You honor me; help me live and work from the peace and balance and compassion from which You live and work and help. Help me in these ways, Mother, so I can at last truly become the instrument you need me to become, the sacred instrument of Your compassion in action that You created me to be, and that I already am in Your holy and illumined eyes.

You are welcome to use this prayer if it moves you; I would be honored. Or you may choose to make up your own prayer, a wonderful and healing practice. After all, you know your own imbalances better than anyone else, so you will write a prayer that is tailored to your specific temperament. Be naked and honest with yourself about the ways you constantly get out of balance; don't judge yourself, but expose the truth of your imbalance to the Beloved.

I have found that I constantly need to correct and align and temper myself and ask for the Mother's help to be less ruthless and careless with myself; whenever I have forgotten to do this, which I have often, the work I do in the world has been edged with anger or infused with exhaustion and I haven't been able to give others my best.

If we, as Sacred Activists, are going to inspire others, it will be by the kindness, balance, truth, and radiance of our presence and of our whole being, by the health and joy we radiate. In order to bring such radiance to others, you need to tend its subtle and tender flame in yourself.

SERVICE TO ALL SENTIENT BEINGS IN YOUR LIFE

I was walking with Father Bede in the grove of tall, ancient trees near his ashram, by the Cauvery River. He said to me, "Everything would change if only we could treat every single being we meet, human or animal, as who they really are—a disguise of God. Your enemy is as much God as you are; the waiter serving you is God; the annoying old woman talking too loudly on the bus is God. The deeper you are taken into the heart of non-dual experience, the greater the tenderness and respect you cannot help feeling for all sentient beings, for you know, not sentimentally but by direct knowledge, that you are one with them in the One." At that moment, a very old peasant woman, carrying some sticks she had gathered by the river, came walking down the path. Father Bede stopped talking, went up to her, bowed slightly to her, and took half of her bundle, giving me some to carry also. The old woman was beside herself with happiness, for, as she explained to us, she had bad arthritis in her hips and knees and walking at all was hard. We walked half a mile with her and when we parted it seemed as if we were all old friends.

This kind of courteous reverence toward others is easier in the slower-paced world of rural India than in our crazed and anxious world where everyone is bearing such a burden of stress. But ever since that holy ordinary walk with Father Bede and the old woman, I have tried to remember that every human being and every animal I meet is the Divine in disguise and that I should treat them with respect. I fail at this often; I get as impatient and judgmental as everyone else. But when I remember and follow this simple yet powerful practice, I find that a light goes on in my heart and I edge closer to experiencing in the ordinary what I have experienced in revelation: that everything and everyone is filled with the Divine Presence, that, in the words of the great Islamic mantra La ilaha il Allah—"there is no God but God."

The service of all sentient beings as being disguises of God is, I believe, one of the great healing powers of Sacred Activism. Performing it humbly in the heart of life allows you to experience more and more strongly three related forces that will strengthen and inspire you—the force of your own innate compassion, the force of the Divine Presence in every being, and the force of the Divine Presence in reality.

I would urge all Sacred Activists in our time to pay special attention to the Divine Presence in all animals. We have made a worldwide concentration camp for animals in which we are not only destroying their habitats, but also killing and slaughtering them in brutal conditions. I am convinced that our treatment of animals is inviting a tsunami of dark karma and that waking up to what we are doing on every level is an important clue for our survival. Next time you see a dog or cat or squirrel, realize that you are seeing the Self in one of its most touching and delightful forms and commit yourself to standing up increasingly for animal rights. You will find that seeing and celebrating the Divine Presence in animals will awaken your desire to eat less meat and to protect the environment. Over time, you will come to know, with a deep and poignant passion, just how much all animals want to communicate with us and how they are waiting for us to be open enough to do so. This will revolutionize your idea of relationship with God and expand it to include the fly buzzing against your windowpane and the green lizard basking on the grass. Knowing that reality offers such a relationship will open you even more intensely to the wonder and miracle of the world and strengthen your resolve to serve it.

Service to all sentient beings starts with your family, friends, and pets. Make a commitment to remember that those whom you deal with intimately are all secretly divine. You will fail in this constantly, as I do. Don't waste time in judging and condemning yourself—that, too, can be a bitter game of the ego—just return to the practice with tenderness and self-forgiveness, and you will see that over time those whom you have to deal with intimately will become more and more precious to you. From this experience of forming increasingly sacred relationships, a wholly new vision of the sacredness of reality will start to be born in you.

But it is not only your intimate circle that needs to be seen and served in this way. In the course of our days we meet all different kinds of people—bus drivers, shopkeepers, waiters, bank tellers, and telephone operators. Remembering to treat everyone with sacred respect is perhaps the most difficult practice for our goal-oriented, self-driven egos; we all tend to feel that it is our needs that are most urgent and important and that others exist only to fulfill them as quickly and efficiently as possible. This is especially true in western societies where nearly everything is based on bottom-line utilitarian efficiency. We are encouraged to see ourselves and everyone else as cogs in a machine that has to be kept working relentlessly at all costs. The price we pay for this feverish coldness is immense; it deadens our souls and fills our bodies with nervous stress. Practicing sacred respect for all others starts to release us from these harsh forces and set us free to be our truest selves. The essence of my vision of Sacred Activism is that the power and effectiveness of our actions in the world depends on the quality of intention we bring to them.

I once met an elevator attendant in a hotel in Arizona. He was old, grizzled, and perky and sported a curled-up Daliesque moustache. He told me that he had once been stuck in the elevator with an extraordinary person in red robes who changed his life. They were together for almost 20 minutes, and the man in red robes treated him with such patience, humor, and consideration that he lost all nervousness, all sense of shame that his lift wasn't working, and started to talk about his family and his life. When the lift finally arrived in the lobby, the man in red robes embraced him warmly and then stepped out smiling to greet a large crowd of people who were waiting for him. It was the Dalai Lama. The attendant told me, "I never felt so loved in my life."

SERVICE TO YOUR LOCAL COMMUNITY

Nothing is more important than restoring public service in our communities. Modern life separates us from each other, and this increases suffering immeasurably. It has never been more essential for all of us to recognize that we are all in the same boat, that our local communities reflect the emotional, physical, social, political, financial problems of the larger world .

Think globally, but act locally. When my friends and pupils who want to help ask me what they should do, I always say the same thing: follow your heartbreak. Determine which one of all the causes in the world really breaks your heart. When you identify this, you have found the cause you will always have the energy and passion to work for. Once you have identified this cause, act immediately in your local community, so your heartbreak doesn't remain abstract but becomes a living force of practical compassion in your daily world.

Let me offer you a practice to help you identify your heartbreak and experience the focus and empowerment it can give you.

Set your alarm clock to wake you up at 3:00 one morning. This early hour of the morning, as many mystical systems know, is a particularly good time to do spiritual work because the noise of the world is hushed and it is easy to feel alone with your spirit and with the Divine. Sit calmly and peacefully on your bed and open your heart, perhaps with a prayer or mantra you love. Only then—when you have grown peaceful and strong—allow yourself to feel the pain of what is happening in the world. Ask yourself: what is the cause of all the causes I care for that breaks my heart the most? When I first did this practice, I discovered that the cause that aroused my deepest heartbreak was the way in which we treat animals. Since then I have done everything I can to advocate animal rights and try to help people become aware of the sacredness of creation.

When, through this practice, you have identified your heartbreak, imagine that your heartbreak has become a torch of flame that guides you down a spiral staircase into a small, dark cave. This small, dark cave is a symbol of your heart center. By the golden light that your heartbreak is emitting, you see that there is a letter on the floor of the cave with your name on it in your own handwriting. Praying for courage and clarity, pick up that letter, open it, and read it. Written in the letter will be your life's purpose, spelling out your particular role in the Birth.

I have taught this practice all over North America and Europe with remarkable results. One woman, passionate about cats, saw that she was called to volunteer in her local animal shelter; a former teacher realized that his passion to teach was as alive in him as ever and decided to become a mentor to four young African American men and help them lift themselves out of the violent life they had fallen into; one middle-aged woman read that she was to help a local women's prison and began giving free meditation classes there two evenings a week; an old Jewish rabbi started to speak for free in high schools about the ancient prophets and the acute modern relevance of their vision of justice.

What is remarkable was that everyone who did this practice and found his or her "mission" said the same thing to me: "Now that I am doing something real in my local community to serve the cause I care most about, I find my life is far happier and the free-floating anxiety about the world that I have been feeling for a long time is beginning to ease." They all told me that starting to "follow their heartbreak" and put compassion into immediate action in their local community had inspired many of their friends to do the same. As the young woman who loves cats said, "Someone has to start. Many people are longing to be of help but don't know what to do or how to do it. When I explained to my friends that I was heartbroken about what is happening to animals and had decided to put my love into practice in the local shelter, they immediately got the connection and started to do their own service in terms of their own temperaments and resources."

I believe that part of what the world crisis is "designed" to do is to break open our hearts to the reality of cruelty and suffering. I believe, too, that if each person were to follow his own private heartbreak and then do something about it in his local community, a great lessening of pain would occur, replaced by an overwhelming surge of hope. The divine heart of the Mother herself is heartbroken at what we are doing to ourselves and Nature; when the image of Mary is seen in mystical apparitions, such as at Lourdes and Fatima, she is often weeping and crying out to us to stop acting in such heartless ways, endangering others and ourselves. Through our own deepest heartbreak, we connect with this divine heartbreak of the Divine Feminine, and it recruits us to do our particular work, then fills us with the passion and hope to undertake it.

I have emphasized strongly here the necessity of "doing," but I also believe it is possible to construct a model of Sacred Activism that can accommodate people of a wide range of dispositions. One alternative that I find helpful and moving was proposed by the Christian contemplative Cynthia Bourgeault. In addition to the model of outward action illumined by heartbreak and fueled by sacred practice, she proposes two other kinds of Sacred Activists: 1) those who pursue a withdrawn, contemplative life but who radiate their energies into the world to protect sentient beings and 2) those who work at the occult level, who are inherently contemplative but seek to alter the course of events by contacting spiritual beings and occult forces and molding them with their contemplative power in ways that secure and safeguard the human future.

SERVICE TO THE GLOBAL COMMUNITY

In this world crisis, every single human being from every walk of life is in danger, and each choice we make affects everyone else. The only possible response to this acute interconnectedness is what the Dalai Lama calls "universal responsibility": the decision to be conscious in the core of our lives of the effect all our choices have on every other being, and so to make all of our choices—economic, social, political—congruent with our most compassionate beliefs.

What does this mean in practice to someone who wants to be a Sacred Activist? It means always remembering to pray for the happiness and safety of all sentient beings, both when you begin your private spiritual practices and when you end them; it means dedicating all merits and benefits of your practice, both at the beginning and at the end, to all other beings everywhere; it means committing to being deeply informed on the major crises afflicting our planet, especially our growing environmental challenges; it means having the integrity to see that your money is not invested in corporations that destroy the environment or exploit sweatshop labor; it means buying a fuel-efficient car and taking as much public transportation as you can; it means becoming aware that our meat-eating habits not only cause great pain to the animals we slaughter, but also engender massive environmental abuse in the clearing of forest for agriculture and so choosing to limit our meat intake or go vegetarian.

It also means honoring our duty as citizens in our various local communities and countries and voting for those officials whom we consider best qualified to safeguard the planet and address the real issues of financial hardship now crowding around us. It means scrutinizing our own consumerist habits: in a time when so many families are going to bed hungry, it is morally imperative to decide to simplify our lives. Finally, it means being strongly critical of any opinion we hear in our private circle that promotes intolerance of any religion or prejudice against any group.

All of this can and should be done without self-righteousness. Who of us, even the most conscious among us, does not collude in some way with the very forces of greed, competition, and exploitation that are destroying the world? Even the Dalai Lama takes planes. Even Mother Teresa got driven around Calcutta in a car. Recognizing this inevitable collusion makes you humbler and kinder and more aware of how hard it can be for many people— for all of us, if we are honest—to make the way we live congruent in every way with what we believe and hope for the future.

The greatest reward of trying to live congruently is that you begin to respect yourself more. A major part of the hopelessness I see everywhere is the unspoken belief that everyone is so involved in the "system" that it is impossible to do something real and useful. This has, of course, some uncomfortable truth in it. It is also true that we still have a great many areas in which we can step up and make choices that make a difference and give us a sense of integrity, which over time empowers us. This sense of empowerment, in both small and large issues, is essential to the success of Sacred Activism. It cannot be given to you, it has to be earned individually. Finding that you can become more congruent in all of your choices restores to you a living sense that things in general can be changed and that conditions in the world can be transformed.

When you fuse together these five forms of service in the core of your life, you begin to discover for yourself the living truth of the Birth that is now breaking out everywhere and of the strength of hope, energy, passion, focus, and joy it can fill you with. As Rumi writes:

> To be born in love
> Is to serve all beings and all creation.
> Real lovers serve ardently, hopefully,
> And in an ecstasy of awe.
> Look for the happiness
> Of the servant of love—
> All the joys of the world are nothing to it.

PART III

To sustain the imperiled and bring order
to chaos is not possible without wisdom.

— LAO-TZU

As the means, so the end.

— MAHATMA GANDHI

CHAPTER 9

THE LAW
OF SACRED
PRACTICE

Sacred Activists cannot begin to live from the depths of Divine
Consciousness and act from the depths of Divine Wisdom and
Compassion without first making the commitment to a daily spiritual discipline. The Jungian analyst Marion Woodman, a pioneer
of the Divine Feminine, once said to me, "Continuing to do pio-
neering sacred work in a world as crazy and painful as ours without constantly grounding yourself in sacred practice would be like
running into a forest fire dressed only in a paper tutu."

When Mahatma Gandhi was asked what helped him persevere
through decades of struggle and defeat, he said prayer and meditation were the keys to his survival. I once asked the Dalai Lama what
gave him the strength to keep on working for the freedom of Tibet,
and he replied, "I begin each day with three hours of meditation and
visualization practices. It is they that give me what little calm and
wisdom and persistence I have." When I met Mother Teresa on
one of her visits to England in the 1970s, I asked her where she
found the faith to go on working day in, day out, with the ill and
abandoned and dying. She replied, "Every morning, whether I am
well or sick, I sit in silence before the Holy Sacrament. I find that

adoration of the Holy Sacrament helps Jesus fill me with everything I will need for the day. And when at the end of the day I am empty, I know from long experience that the next day I will be filled again." I have met several people who knew Martin Luther King, Jr. They all told me that the foundation of his heroic work for peace and nonviolence was a profound prayer practice that kept him buoyant and full of energy through all the betrayals and defeats he endured. One person told me, "Martin was a man whose inner being was relentlessly sculpted by prayer; this is what gave him both the passion that kept flaming from him even in the midst of despair and the peace and humor he radiated even in the midst of the most harrowing circumstances."

One of the contemporary Sacred Activists I admire most is Julia Butterfly Hill. I sat on a panel with her once and she moved me deeply with her inner and outer beauty and the integrity that shone from her, like light from a diamond. When Julia was living in the towering redwood tree she called Luna to prevent it and the ancient forest around it from being cut down, she learned, she told me, not only how to meditate but also to connect "with the inner peace and strength of Luna herself, the strength and peace of the sacred force that lived inside her." It was through connecting with this force that she was able to stay calm and concentrated on her mission even in her most difficult moments. When I myself was enduring repeated death threats and harassment of all kinds after I left my guru, there were many months in which I could only find the strength to go on testifying in public to what had happened by saying the Hail Mary over and over again. It was in this time that I came to learn how impassioned and sincere prayer can fill you with a courage and energy beyond ordinary human capacity.

From my own experience of being a Sacred Activist, I have discovered that four kinds of sacred practice are essential for a joyful embodiment of Divine Love and Wisdom in action: cool practices, warm practices, prayer, and sacred body practices.

COOL PRACTICES

Practices such as simple meditation, walking meditation, chanting, and saying the name of God peacefully in the heart help us keep calm and grounded and allow us to experience the transcendent peace of our inner divine being in the middle of the storms of our world. The Divine, as all mystics know, is calm, serene, and blissful in its essential Being. The cool practices enable you to stay connected to, and constantly be upheld by, this calm serenity and bliss. This is especially important for Sacred Activists with my kind of passionate, impetuous nature; the dark side of passion and impetuousness are anger, judgmental ferocity, and isolating self-righteousness. These, I have found, can be transformed only by constant immersion in the cool practices. Working with the cool practices steadies me, allows me to see clearly when I am succumbing to panic or fury, and gives me the kind of detachment and peace of spirit that are not natural to me but that I have begun to acquire through daily discipline.

I have found, too, that one of the potential drawbacks of caring passionately about the future of the planet is that it has often made me impatient: I am impatient by nature, as anyone who has met me knows all too well, and all my life have struggled with a kind of impatient imperiousness that demands immediate results. Nearly all the activists I have met suffer from a variation of this impatience, and I have sympathy for them. While such impatience can in certain circumstances get necessary things done quickly and efficiently, it can also sever you from the more peaceful and serene rhythms of authentic divine action and cause unnecessary suffering when things do not go well. This is of no use whatsoever in the rigorous conditions of the real world.

I spoke of this once with Bernard Kouchner, the co-founder of Doctors Without Borders, whose fiery temperament I recognized as like my own. When I described to him how much I needed the "cool" practices to counterbalance the passion and wildness that are natural to me, he laughed. "Without meditation I think I would have committed murder or suicide," he said, "and that, I hope you agree, would have been a pity."

The transcendent realism of the I Ching expresses the power and truth of the cool practices in the commentary on Hexagram 52, "Gen: keeping still, mountain." In the explanation of the hexagram we find this instruction: "keeping his back still so that he no longer feels his body." The commentary tells us that this phrase signifies the end and the beginning of all movement. The back is named because in the back are located all the nerve fibers that mediate movement. If the movement is brought to a standstill, the ego with its restlessness disappears. The commentary adds "when a man has thus become calm, he may turn to the outside world. He no longer sees in it the struggle and tumult of individual beings, and therefore he has that true peace of mind which is needed for understanding the great laws of the universe and for acting in harmony with them. Whoever acts from these deep levels makes no mistakes."

Nearly all of the mistakes I have made have been because I was too undisciplined to "act from these deep levels." Over years of causing offense by my unchecked intensity, I have, I hope, begun to learn my lesson. The only criticism Father Bede ever gave me, which I have tried never to forget, was: "Sometimes, I expect you are 'too much' even for yourself. You will always need to practice peace. Remember that the flame of a candle can only burn and continue to burn so long as it is fed by wax or oil. That wax or oil is inner peace. That is why Saint Francis chose in his prayer to ask to be made an instrument of peace, and that is why perhaps the greatest gift of the Christ consciousness is, as Jesus promised us, the 'peace beyond understanding.'"

WARM PRACTICES

Cool practices, while basic to the Path of Radical Embodiment, are not the only practices we need in the turmoil of the world; we must also know how to access the fire energies of the heart, Warm practices—such as Sufi heart practices, Hinayana Buddhist practices of Metta, loving-kindness to all beings, and passionate devotional chanting—are essential to keeping the heart center open and flowing with the passion of compassion. They enable the joyful energy of Divine Love to remain alive and vibrant in you through times of frustration, disappointment, defeat, and anguish.

If you practice the cool practices exclusively, you can become, as a Buddhist environmental activist once said to me, "too damn heavenly and serene to be of any earthly use." The peace, serenity, and bliss that the cool practices provide can be used by the subtle ego as a drug to mask the agony of the world and the urgent need for action to remedy that agony. In our time, most seekers have fallen prey to this temptation, which, when you succumb to it, creates a false detachment from reality and a subtle arrogance. This is especially dangerous for Sacred Activists, who need to bring about within themselves a difficult Sacred Marriage of serenity and urgency, inner peace and passionately compassionate energy. For the work of the Birth, you need both sacred peace and sacred passion. You need to be able to integrate and unite, at ever greater and subtler depths, the essential peace of Divine Being with the essential radiant and holy passion of Divine Becoming, the transcendent Wisdom Serenity of the Father with the ever-flowing Love Fire of the Mother. Only such a Sacred Marriage can help you become more richly, wisely, and completely the conduit of the full Divine Consciousness, with access to both its serene detachment and its focused power. As Kabir wrote, "My father is the transcendent Absolute, and my mother is the embodied Godhead. I am their Divine child, dancing in the burning-ground of life with the Father's peace and the Mother's wild love."

One of the limitations of the patriarchal religions and mystical systems is that, in their fear of "feminine" passion, they overstress the primacy of the cool practices. In my 20 years of experience as a spiritual teacher in the West, I have found that much New Age work has focused on the "cool" as well. In many cases this has led to what I can only call a "lopsided awakening," one that, while it may put you in touch with Divine Being, with healing and sometimes transformative results, does not help you access the passion and intensity that you also need to fuel sacred action. Rumi was once asked what characterized a true lover of God; he replied, "The power of passion that comes from heartbreak and the peace of serenity that comes from surrender." Tibetan master Nyoshul Khenpo expresses this union of peaceful wisdom and passionate compassion and the "skillful means" that are engendered by it in this way:

> An effortless compassion can arise for all beings who have not realized their true nature. So limitless is it that if tears could express it, you would cry without end. Not only compassion, but tremendous skillful means can be born when you realize the nature of the mind. Also you are naturally liberated from all suffering and fear . . . If you were to speak of the joy and bliss that arises from this realization, it is said by the Buddhas that if you were to gather all the glory, enjoyment, pleasure, and happiness of the world and put it all together, it would not approach one tiny fraction of the bliss that you experience upon realizing the nature of mind.

The bliss that Nyoshul Khenpo is celebrating is what some mystics call the Great Bliss. Inspired by this Great Bliss that is a fusion of the dynamic opposites within the Divine itself, the Sacred Activist can endure and risk anything for the victory of compassion and justice in the world. Rumi calls this "the wine that keeps the warrior lucidly drunk and brave in the heat of battle." If you want to experience what this fusion of sacred peace and sacred passion can make possible, watch the footage of Martin Luther King, Jr., delivering his great "I Have a Dream" speech on the steps of the Lincoln Memorial. King is in calm possession of his soul, rooted in his body, and utterly on fire with pure prophetic ecstasy and passion. This fusion of opposites enables him not only to deliver a message of transforming truth, but to be a living sign of its power.

Another crucial reason for doing the warm practices is that they allow you to keep your heart open when you are threatened by "compassion fatigue." The world we have created out of our ignorance and greed is aflame with pain; it is very hard to remain open to this suffering without falling asleep or lapsing into denial. In developing the vision of Sacred Activism I have presented here, I have often had to face despair and fight the urge not to feel the reality of the Death in all its horror. While I need the cool practices constantly, I find I need the warm practices, too, to help me endure heartbreak long enough to discover the treasure of compassionate passion-energy hidden in its core.

As Rumi wrote: "Wherever you may be, in whatever situation or circumstance you may find yourself, strive always to be a lover, and a passionate lover. Once you possess your heart in love, you will always be a lover, in the tomb, at the Resurrection, and in Paradise forever. Sow wheat and wheat will grow; wheat will flourish in the fields, and bread will glow in the oven."

Warm practices are what enable you to keep the bread of passionate compassion glowing in the oven of the heart.

THE PRACTICE OF PRAYER

When I was a young, disillusioned Fellow of All Souls College, Oxford, I had the good luck to meet an old abbess of a cloistered order of nuns housed in the middle of the city. She was in her '80s, funny, joyful, and robust with the kind of formidable no-nonsense robustness that English women of a certain age and training are famous for. In meeting her, I felt I was meeting a being like Teresa of Avila, who combined the loftiest mystical ecstasies with a passion for eating partridge and a relish for the odd glass of wine or two. She took me under her shrewd and capacious wing, and we had many conversations whose essential wisdom has unfolded in me over the decades since her death. One conversation I remember particularly. We were standing at the great bay window in her room that looked out on one of the busiest streets in the city. It was a depressing February afternoon, gray and somber, and everyone in the street seemed sad.

"Do you know what I would love to be able to give to every single person out there?" she asked me.

Wisely, I said I had no idea.

"Not just a belief in but an experience of the beauty and power of prayer. You know, as a young nun I used to think privately that prayer was grossly overrated, even though I had chosen to be a nun in a closed order devoted to prayer. There were years when, every time I knelt to pray, I would wonder, 'Why on earth am I doing this? Am I only in here out of fear, out of a desire to escape the hurly-burly of the world?'"

The idea of a woman like her being intimidated by any kind of "hurly-burly" made me smile. She caught my smile and laughed.

"I know you see me as a kind of holy battle-axe, and I am. But the strength and force you love in me—and I know you do, otherwise you wouldn't keep coming around—was not native to me. When I was young I was a frail, neurotic, overexcited little thing, easily depressed and a bother to myself. The slightest bad news from the outside world would make me call out to Jesus, 'Take me now, Lord, I can't stand any more of this madness.' But over long years, a practice of prayer grew strong in me, and the weakness in me became fortified."

I had never heard the word fortified used with such exuberance, and I smiled again.

She gave me one of her well-known piercing looks. "I chose the word 'fortified' carefully because that is what sustained prayer gives you—a kind of inner fort in which you can stand tall and from which you can withstand the 'slings and arrows of outrageous fortune.'" Her two great passions in life were Jesus, whom she always referred to in the present tense as if she had just come from talking with him, and Shakespeare, whom, next to Jesus, she considered the greatest spiritual genius of humanity. Most of the saints she had little time for ("a querulous sin-obsessed bunch, most of them, if you ask me. Didn't they know that God is joy?").

I asked her what her long practice of prayer had given her. "Three things," she replied immediately, "and they are linked.

Strength, because when you develop the habit of prayer you tap into the strength of God. Certainty of the Divine Presence, because when you pray long and hard enough you come to know without a shadow of a doubt that the Great Love is always listening. Patience, because sometimes, being human, you pray for the wrong thing or for what would not be good for you, and the No! you get from God is also an answer that you have to accept and work with in deeper and more selfless prayer."

She fell silent and I saw that her eyes, the blue of robins' eggs, had filled with tears.

Then she turned to me and said, "Why on earth do you think the Blessed Virgin, whenever and wherever she appears, begs us to pray, to pray constantly and fervently, for everything we need to do the divine work and for the peace of the world?"

I said caustically, "Not knowing the Blessed Virgin personally, I have no idea."

"Well, I do know the Blessed Virgin personally; if I didn't by now, at 83, after 60 years of banging at her door, I'd be even more of a lunatic than I am. I'll tell you why she asks us to pray. It sure as hell isn't because she's pious and wants to see everyone on their knees, with their hands folded sweetly, muttering half-understood words to cheer themselves up. The Virgin doesn't give a fig for superficial formal piety. If she's anything, she's practical. She's a woman and a mother, after all. She asks us to pray because it works. Over time, sustained, humble, passionate prayer can not only move mountains, it can make them dance and clap their hands.

"The Virgin is asking the whole world to pray because she knows what a terrible mess we have gotten ourselves into, and she knows that prayer can be a channel of the most overwhelming Divine Grace that even, at the two-minutes-before-midnight place we are in, can transform everything.

"The Virgin knows this, as everyone can come to know it, through personal experience. It was her power of prayer that made her humble and surrendered enough to 'receive' the Christ and birth him; it was the power of prayer that gave her the strength to endure what she had to bringing up a divine being in a world full of spiteful nutcases; it was the power of prayer that gave her the love to let him go about his mission and leave her protection when he had to; it was the power of prayer that held her and kept her standing through all the horror of the Crucifixion; it was the power of her prayer, what Leo X (one of my least favorite popes) called 'The Virgin's unimaginable intensity of prayer' that called down the flames of Pentecost. You don't think it was the disciples who called down those flames, do you? They were a pretty sorry bunch on the whole. Dear boy, the Virgin asks the world to pray because it is through the power of prayer that she, a humble Jewish woman, became, over time, one with the Motherhood of God, which is why, when the Divine Mother tries to wake us up to where we are and what we now need to be and do, she needs the Virgin as her 'foreign minister.'"

No one had ever spoken to me about prayer or the Virgin in such a way, and for once I was too moved and bewildered to speak. The abbess said, "And when are you going to take the power of prayer seriously? Reading the mystical classics is all well and good and having the odd experience is nice and dandy. But it is when you get down to the nitty-gritty of constant prayer that you are beginning the real work. Let us start right now."

She fell on her knees. "Come on, big boy, get on your knees. You're not going to let me kneel here all alone, are you?"

"My God, you're ruthless," I said.

"Yes, I am," she said softly, delighted. "I'm an ill old woman and I don't have much time and I want to see you safe before I go. You have so many gifts but you lack the humility to ask for what you need and the faith to believe that prayer can over time have results. And without that humility and that faith everything you try and do will be half-assed."

I joined her on my knees skeptically, a little put out by the accuracy of her diagnosis. We prayed silently together for 20 minutes. For the first 15 I felt annoyed and impatient. Then quite suddenly a wave of joy and peace swept over me and seemed to possess not only my mind and heart but my body too. It was an astonishing experience and one that permanently altered what little I had known and understood about prayer.

"You see?" she said, rubbing my cheek.

"Yes, I see. I'm so sorry—"

She cut me short with a wild laugh.

"Oh, for God's sake, don't be sorry. Don't be sorry you didn't know; be glad—no, be wild with joy—that you are beginning to. Now I have to go. One of my nuns has been making quite a fuss about nothing, and I have to give her quite a severe dressing down, which I might enjoy rather too much, if I don't restrain myself."

All the teachers of all the traditions I have studied with have told me, in their own way, what the abbess told me. Rumi wrote: "Prayer is not just for the set times of kneeling and bowing; the real challenge of prayer is to prolong that state of absorption always, to keep the heart in a constant fire of adoration, whether you are asleep or awake, writing or reading. In all circumstances and every situation, see that you never wander from God's hand. What is said in the Koran, 'they continue at their prayers,' should also describe you . . . Don't ever be too proud or too afraid to present your needs to God; never, for one moment, be without remembrance of Him. The remembrance of God is force, power, strength, and endurance; it is feathers and wings to the bird of the spirit."

It was when I came to my own Dark Night of the soul during the years after leaving my guru that I experienced the power of prayer at a level and intensity I had never known. When you come to extreme suffering, your mind can be too invaded by anguish to allow you to meditate and your heart too full of fear and horror to do any of the warm practices more than perfunctorily. In fact, one of the characteristics of the Dark Night, as Saint John of the Cross and the Sufi mystics remind us, is that your previous inner experiences of the Divine may no longer be available to you and the spiritual practices you have lived your inner life by may no longer work. This has, of course, a divine purpose and meaning—to drive you deeper and deeper into surrender and ever more accurate and unsparing knowledge of your own helplessness without the direct

constant grace of God. Jesus did not meditate in the Garden of
Gethsemane; he sweated blood and wept and prayed; anyone who
comes to his own Gethsemane will find that in that harrowing
garden, prayer will be his deepest support.

When I saw Thuksey Rinpoche in that last summer in Ladakh
when he was dying from diabetes, I noticed that he was in a constant state of prayer; whenever he was not teaching, or exhausting
himself encouraging and cajoling us, he would immediately pick
up his rosary and chant in his sonorous bass voice, "Om mani
padme hum." When Bede was enduring the long agony of his
last illness, he would pray for hours on end, sometimes silently
and sometimes out loud, the Jesus Prayer that he had loved and
used all his life: "Lord Jesus Christ have mercy on me." On my
last visit to Istanbul, I met an old and holy Sufi woman who had
just been diagnosed with terminal bone cancer. I asked her how
she could remain so happy and concentrated. "It is simple," she
said. "I don't do any complicated practices any more. The pain is
too great. I just say at every moment, inwardly, 'La ilaha il allah,'
there is no other God but God. It is only now that I am beginning
to understand just how deep a grace streams to us through those
divine syllables." And she broke down and wept, not tears of pain,
but tears of abandoned gratitude.

Sometimes when I speak to Sacred Activists of the power of
prayer, they look at me a little askance, as if to say, "You may think
it works for you, but I frankly do not believe it." Even when I speak
about the extensive modern research that shows that prayer can
have observable and extraordinary effects over long distances, they
look skeptical. Many have been "burned" by the hypocritical and
sometimes hysterical piety of the traditions they are fleeing from.
If I can persuade them to try prayer, and try it sincerely, they often
write to me: "Thank God I trusted you enough to begin to pray. I
cannot begin to describe what strength I have derived from it."

A couple of years ago I spoke to a group of AIDS volunteers
going to Darfur. I said to them, "What you are going to see and
feel will make most kinds of meditation hard to sustain. If you
can choose a short, simple prayer and keep saying it in your heart

whatever you are witnessing and going through, I swear to you that will be of more help than you can imagine now."

One of the volunteers, a beautiful green-eyed French woman, came up to me and said contemptuously, "Do you really believe saying a few syllables over and over again will help me bear what I will have to bear?"

"Yes, I do," I said.

"Have you ever had to pick up the bloody pieces of a child exploded by a bomb or cradle a five-year-old girl after she has been gang-raped?"

"No," I said, "but I have come to some terrible dark places and in those I have found prayer has been as essential to my survival as breathing." She looked at me as if I had slapped her, then stalked off.

Three months later I got a letter from her from Darfur: "I didn't like you or what you said or the way you said it. But I came to such an abyss of despair and such a depth of exhaustion that one night, slightly drunk and at the end of my last rope, I thought, well, hell, why don't I just try praying? I don't know if there is any God or, if there is any God, that he or she or it is listening anymore, but maybe just talking to myself in the dark will keep me from jumping out the window. So I started to say the only prayer I knew—the Hail Mary. I had been regularly beaten by sadistic nuns at one of those convent boarding schools with hard beds and peeling white walls that smell perpetually of stale laundry and soap; at first I rebelled and deliberately mixed up the words and thought myself an idiot. But I continued. I don't know why I continued, but I did. Perhaps I was at last desperate enough to at least want to believe in something. Perhaps, too, my pride had been broken enough to begin in me the kind of 'humility' you described, which frankly nauseated me at the time.

"Nothing miraculous happened; I am clearly not Bernadette. But after half an hour I felt peaceful and actually able to get some rest. I had not slept for more than an hour or two for months, it seemed. The things you see here could keep you from sleep for a lifetime. But that night, I slept until morning. And when I awoke I found myself saying, 'Hail Mary, full of grace', and for the first time I broke into tears. When you are a nurse dealing all the time with atrocity, you can't help hardening your heart. Your heart turns to black stone. The words of that silly old prayer—as I had always thought it—and the tears they evoked in me beyond my will cracked open the black stone my heart had become. Since then, shamefacedly and amazed at myself, I have found myself using it often every day, even singing it sometimes (God, you should hear my singing). I shall never become a Christian or 'pious,' and I'm still not sure who 'Mary' is. What I am increasingly sure of, though—despite everything my well-honed Sorbonne-trained mind tells me—is that there is Something, some great mysterious Love that is listening, and listening—God knows why—to me, to me personally, or listening in me. I don't know anything really, but I trust now and I find I am able to work more calmly and without the rage and despair that so exhausted me. So I suppose I have to say to you, thank you. Thank you for being so annoying and imprinting some of your passion on my heart, despite my 'better judgment.'"

Of all the letters I have received from activists in the field, this is the one I treasure the most.

Prayer is an inexhaustible subject, but there are two things in particular I want to add in the context of Sacred Activism. The first is that I have found praying together with others is even more powerful than praying alone; one of my dreams is to set up prayer circles everywhere for Sacred Activists to pray for peace, for the hearts of the powerful to be opened, for quick and brave legislation on the environment, for a revolution in energy policy, for the awakening of the human heart to the agony of animals, and for the strength to go on being Sacred Activists in a world where progress often arrives painfully slow and soaked in ambiguity or blood.

The other kind of prayer that I find sustains my hope is what in the Catholic Church is known as intercessory prayer—prayer that intercedes for the healing or well-being of others. Because I have felt its effects when it has been prayed for me, and because I have known its power in the lives of those I have prayed for, I find myself using it more and more, and with more and more simple faith. Father Bede once said to me, "Not one prayer is ever wasted; not one loving thought sent in faith toward another human being is ever useless. When you know that, you know that you can always be of help."

There are a few beings on the earth, I believe, who have reached such a humble level of union with God that what they will in prayer is granted, because what they will and what the Divine wills is the same. I feel that Father Bede in his last years was often in such a surrendered and empowered state. Because of my experience of him and the grace his love and prayers for me keep streaming into my life, I believe that one of the greatest powers an increasingly divinized humanity will have is the power to work what are now called, probably inaccurately, "miracles" through the power of prayer. This is one of the holiest and most practical reasons for striving to make as much progress on the Path of Radical Embodiment as you can. Just imagine what a growing number of Sacred Activists acting humbly within the world and infused with such a grace of power could make possible.

There is an old Jewish myth that claims that the world is allowed to keep going because of the righteousness and selfless prayer of 36 men and women. Every Sacred Activist who has truly seen what is now at stake and what is now possible should try to find the courage to pray perhaps the most dangerous and transforming prayer of all—to join and swell their company. As an old Hasidic rabbi who loved this story once said to me in Jerusalem, "I think, my dear Andrew, that in the world as it is now, God probably needs a lot more than 36 to keep us going. What about 36,000?"

What about 36,000 indeed!

SACRED BODY PRACTICES

In *The Supramental Manifestation,* Sri Aurobindo writes: "In the spiritual tradition the body has been regarded as an obstacle incapable of spiritualization or transmutation and a heavy weight holding the soul to earthly nature and preventing its ascent either to spiritual fulfillment in the Supreme or to the dissolution of its individual being in the Supreme. But while this conception of the role of the body in our destiny is suitable enough for a *sadhana* [discipline] that sees earth only as a field of the ignorance and the earth-life a preparation for a saving withdrawal . . . it is insufficient for one which conceives of a divine life on earth and liberation of earth-nature itself as part of a total purpose of the embodiment of the spirit here. If a total transformation of the being is our aim, a transformation of the body must be an indispensable part of it; without that no full divine life is possible."

Later in the same work, Sri Aurobindo describes, from the depths of his own experience, what such a transformed body would be and feel like:

> The body could become a revealing vessel of a supreme beauty and bliss, casting the light of the spirit radiating from it as a lamp reflects and diffuses the luminosity of its indwelling flame, carrying in itself the beatitude of the spirit, its joy of the seeing mind, its joy of life and spiritual happiness, the joy of matter released into a spiritual consciousness and thrilled with a constant ecstasy.

Perhaps the most important clue to the embodiment and integration of mystical consciousness with all aspects of life and sacred action is to understand, revere, and celebrate the inherent sacredness of your body. Knowing that your body is sacred leads to several interlinked initiations in the heart of ordinary existence; it makes you grateful for the blessing of being alive, conscious that all life is the glowing manifestation of spirit, aware of the holiness of other sentient beings, and more alert to the divine splendor of creation.

The Law of Sacred Practice

These interlinked initiations in turn lead to an inward trans-formation that over time comes to reflect itself in every thought and action. Being conscious of the sacredness of the body slowly turns the whole of life into an experience of feast and celebration; every walk or meal or deep sleep or joy at a flower becomes a form of praise and prayer. Being conscious of the holiness of the bod-ies of other sentient beings makes you instinctively more sensi-tive and protective toward them and breeds what Buddha called "a loving harmlessness" in the core of your being. To see, know, and feel, through understanding the sacredness of your own body, the sacredness of the entire creation—from the gazelle to the gray whale to the Himalayas—awakens a passion for God in all forms of life and a practical resolution to do everything in your power to protect Nature.

In a deep sense, our contemporary crisis is a crisis of the body. Our inability to bless our own holiness, to see the infinite beauty of our own and others' bodies, and to see what Blake called "a world in a grain of sand" has blinded us to the Light that lives in each of our cells and in each being and thing that surrounds us.

For a Sacred Activist, committed to embodying Wisdom and Love in action, sacred body practices such as yoga, tai chi, and qi gong are, I have found, essential for three reasons: it is impos-sible to sustain the intensity of service required of us if we do not have strong, healthy bodies; the experience of living both a personal and a collective Dark Night is fierce on both the mind and body, and if the physical body is not kept in optimum health and strength it may buckle under the pressures it will endure; and it is impossible to embody the Birth without working hard and joyfully to make your physical being as supple as possible to the divine energies that descend and those they awaken in you.

Most of the Sacred Activists I know have the same trouble in being attentive to their bodies as I have had and still have. This is because, as Sacred Activists, we inherit both the old spiritual dis-missals of the body and the tendencies of most activists in general to believe that paying attention to their bodies is narcissistic and self-indulgent, something they have no time for in their urgent and righteous passion to get things done. This is perhaps the main reason why Sacred Activists everywhere suffer from so much stress, exhaustion, and burnout and why many of our decisions lack the wisdom and maturity they would have if they radiated from grounded health and not nervous anxiety.

After I returned form my father's deathbed with the vision of the Christ inside me, I flung myself into my teaching with a passion and urgency that came from seeing what was at stake. I was so consumed by what I felt I had to communicate that I neglected my body and came near, on several occasions, to physical collapse. It wasn't only that I was treating my body as an annoyance; it was also that the passion I so wanted to express, because it was not as embodied as it could be, exhausted and riled me and sometimes offended others.

A great friend and master yoga teacher, Karuna Erickson, came up after a Rumi class I gave and said to me, "You are not in your body. Your passion will burn you up if you do not ground it in your body. Sometimes when I watch you give yourself so totally to what you are trying to say without being rooted in your body, I think that if you don't have a serious physical discipline soon, you will die." I love Karuna, and I knew she was telling me the truth. I had been wondering for a while why I felt so burned out and sometimes so dissociated from the people I was addressing. Now I understood that if I wasn't looking after my body I would always live on the edge of burning out, and if I wasn't more grounded and embodied, a certain human warmth and tenderness would be lacking in both what I said and the way I said it.

Karuna's frankness deepened my admiration for her and I became her pupil, as she had been mine. Over the next five years, working quietly and secretly, mostly in her community in Nelson, British Columbia, Karuna and I evolved together what we called Heart Yoga—a practice for Sacred Activists that marries traditional asanas with meditation and visualization and conscious invocation of the Divine Light into the body.

Karuna and I have taught hundreds of Sacred Activists since then and the feedback has been humbling in its fervor and gratitude. One activist for animal rights wrote to me, "I had been doing yoga for years but sporadically and without much enthusiasm. What your and Karuna's return of yoga to its mystical origins and your conscious union of yoga with simple mystical exercises has opened up for me is a joy and peace that I have never experienced before in the body and a supple subtle strength that now permeates everything I do. I find I not only have more energy for my work but more *joy* in it."

The other spiritual physical discipline I especially love, and pursue myself, is sacred dance. I have loved to dance ever since I was a small child, when, my mother tells me, I used to dance all the time, sometimes imitating the intricate hand gestures of the Indian goddesses, rather to the embarrassment of my policeman father. All through my 20s and 30s I would dance whenever the occasion arose—at tea dances on Fire Island with my best friend, Chris, and in a series of nightclubs in Paris and New York. One of the things that attracted me so deeply to Rumi was that he, too, loved to express his joy and realization in dancing—to the scandal of the staid Islamic authorities of Konya. Rumi knew that the whole universe and every atom in it is dancing around the Secret Sun of the Beloved, and the dance he evolved with his teacher, Shams, was later formulated more precisely by his son, Sultan Valad. This "dance of the dervishes," as it is popularly known, is for me the most sublime form of sacred dance ever created.

I have tried traditional dervish "whirling," but I am too clumsy and uncoordinated to perform it with any kind of grace. Fifteen years ago I met the great modern pioneer of sacred dance Gabrielle Roth; we became dear friends fast, and I was moved and impressed both by the austere radiance of her presence and by the subtle spiritual power of her work.

By working with Karuna and Gabrielle I have immeasurably deepened both my respect for and my enjoyment of my body, and although I still have to remind myself not to neglect it, I am far more contentedly embodied at 56 than I ever was in my youth. And over time this new physical joy in myself—and the strength that comes with it—has made my whole style of teaching warmer and more intimate, as well as giving me the stamina to keep up the schedule my activism in the world demands. I find, too, that as my realization of the One Consciousness deepens through grace, I can sustain states of peace and bliss longer and feel them more richly and intimately in my body, and that although I am far from the glorious ideal that Sri Aurobindo describes, I know now that it is not a poetic fantasy but a reality that continued work on my mystical and physical development will continue to unfold in me.

So to all Sacred Activists I would say—please don't wait as I did to plunge into a sacred physical discipline. If neither yoga nor sacred dance attracts you, there are a host of others to choose from—perhaps the greatest gift of the New Age is the plethora of different forms of sacred body practice it has brought within every seeker's reach. Make a commitment to find which one, or which combination, fits you, then stick to it. You are not being selfish in giving attention to your body in this way; in fact, you are preparing it for greater and greater openness to divine joy and peace and, eventually, for a subtler divinization. Through an increasingly divinized body the light of Divine Grace can stream far more effectively, as sun can pass more purely and powerfully through clean glass.

If you combine cool and warm practice with a disciplined prayer and sacred body practice, what you will create for yourself is an holistic and integrated way of aligning yourself constantly with the birthing energies of the One; you will be feeding yourself more and more strength and joy and opening yourself up more and more to the empowering grace of the Divine.

IN PRACTICE

Now I would like to offer one practice that I love from each category of sacred practice.

The Law of Sacred Practice

A Cool Practice: The Chanting of Om

Chanting is one of the most effective and exhilarating ways of raising your entire being into receptivity and joy. All the major mystical traditions have used it: ancient Hindu rishis developed intricate chants to embody mantras in waves of transformative sacred sound; Sufi mystics have set passages from the Koran or love poems by Rumi or Hafiz to chant-like melodies that exalt both listener and singer; many Christian monastic orders—notably, of course, the Carmelites, Cistercians, and Benedictines—have kept alive the tradition of Gregorian chant and its power to open the whole psyche to the vibratory peace of the Infinite.

You don't have to have a strong singing voice or any musical talent to discover the power of chanting for yourself. You can derive a great deal of comfort and inspiration from chanting in simple ways that have strength, beauty, and dignity.

Sit in your chosen place and, as always, dedicate the practice you are about to do to the liberation of all sentient beings. Then meditate silently on the divine significance of the sacred syllable *om*. Here's how it was defined in ancient India, in a passage from the Chandogya Upanishad:

This [om] is the essence of essences, the highest, the eighth
rung,
Venerated above all that human beings hold holy.
Om is the self of all. . . .
With the word *om* we say "I agree"
And with *om* we fulfill desires.
With *om*, we recite, we give direction,
We sing aloud the honor of that Word
The key to the three kinds of knowledge.

A similar passage is found in the Mandukya Upanishad:

The mantram [*om*] is the bow, the aspirant
Is the arrow, and the Lord the target.

Now draw the bowstring of meditation
And hitting the target be one with him.

As Lama Govinda tells us in his *Foundatons of Tibetan Mysticism*, "The sound-values of *om* and their symbolic interpretation [in the Upanishads] are described in the following manner: 'O' is a combination of 'A' and 'U'; the whole syllable . . . consists of three elements . . . A-U-M. Since *om* is the expression of the highest faculty of consciousness, these three elements are explained accordingly as three planes of consciousness: 'A' as the waking consciousness (*jagrat*), 'U' as the dream-consciousness (*svapna*), and 'M' as the consciousness during deep sleep (*turiya*) on the fourth plane, beyond words and concepts—the consciousness of the fourth dimension."

When you come to chant *om*, then, believe and know that you are chanting the most sacred syllable, one that corresponds to the most intimate and holy sound of the cosmos. Believe and know that you are chanting at once the sound of your own inmost Divine Consciousness, the sound that the entire creation is always resonating to, and the sound that the Godhead makes as it creates reality. A sweet old Hindu priest in Tanjore once told me, before we chanted *om* together in the twilight in one of the halls of the Shiva temple, "Always remember that when you chant *om* you are yourself one vibrating note of the always-silent and always-sounding *om* sounding *om* back to Itself. If you chant in this all-embracing way, you will very soon come to have an experience of nonduality." The truth of what I was told on that evening has been revealed to me in many subsequent meditations; it will undoubtedly be revealed to you if you approach this practice with sincerity, knowledge, and real devotion.

Let us return to the actual practice now. When you have spent a few minutes meditating on the sacred significance of *om,* slowly begin to chant it. Use one of the lower notes in your vocal register; *om* should never be chanted too high, because that diminishes its power. Find and hold a note not too far away from the natural note your speaking voice makes when it is speaking tenderly and raptly.

The Law of Sacred Practice

Don't vary the note as you chant *om* again and again. Try to always sound the *om* with the same amount of breath and vocal power. You will find that if you do, the repetition of the same sonorous pitch and sound will calm your whole being and make it receptive to joy. It will also encourage a kind of selflessness that makes the cosmic dimensions of *om* more accessible; if you are concentrating even slightly on how you sound or on the "beauty" of the chant, your self-consciousness will dilute its transformative power.

Om should be chanted in three parts (A-U-M), as Lama Govinda explains, with equal time given to each part. Traditionally, *ah* is chanted in the region of the navel, *oo* in the sternum, and *mm* in the throat.

When you come to chant the last syllable, *mm*, with closed lips, you will become aware of how millions of cells have been awakened in your body by the sacred syllable. After each chanted *om*, savor the ringing silence that follows and the way your whole being resonates with it. At the end of the practice session, chant four long slow *oms*, directing your intention to each of the four directions of the universe and saying silently:

> By the power of this *om* may all creatures to the east of
> me be liberated.
> By the power of this *om* may all creatures to the west be
> liberated.
> By the power of this *om* may all creatures to the south be
> liberated.
> By the power of this *om* may all creatures to the north be
> liberated.

As the last sacred act of the practice, believe and know that your chanting of *om* during the session has transformed your entire body, speech, mind, and heart into an *om*, silently sounding together with the *om* of the universe and radiating Divine Light throughout the cosmos. Rest in the great joy and peace that this recognition brings.

A Warm Practice: Tonglen (Giving and Receiving)

The heart practice that I most recommend for Sacred Activists is the one I have used every day since I was taught it by Thuksey Rinpoche in Ladakh. Tonglen—the practice of giving and receiving—is one of Tibetan Buddhism's most precious gifts to the world. It is a very holy and powerful practice that can help anyone stay open to, and expand, his or her innate tendency to be compassionate. The great mystics of all traditions remind us that at the core of our nature lies a divine capacity for love. Tonglen helps us discover, sustain, expand, and develop this capacity until it becomes the ruling force of our whole being. It can help you learn how strong your own inner power of love and compassion really is and then how transformative and healing it can be, both for you and for others.

The guiding principle of tonglen is simple: in the course of the practice, you take on the pain, terror, and sadness of others and then give out all peace, all love, all help, all possible forms of healing. As you breathe in, you breathe in all suffering; as you breathe out, you breathe out all peace.

There is nothing to fear; the pain, terror, and sadness you take on in this practice will not destroy you. On the contrary, by determining calmly and consciously to take on the sufferings of others, you will wear away your attachment to your false self, the false self that is the source of all our aggression, illusion, and ignorance and that protects itself by self-absorbed hardheartedness and denial. By constantly intending to embrace and transmute the pain of others, you will be constantly wearing away everything in you that considers you alone, separate, or uninvolved, and so you will be uncovering ever more clearly your true divine nature. Every time you do this practice with a sincere intention to help another person who is in pain, you will also be offering up your own separate false self for transformation and so taking a step toward your own liberation from illusion. The greatest mystics of all traditions remind us that progress along the Path is best gauged by growth in selflessness and humility. As a Tibetan mystic, Shantideva, wrote:

The Law of Sacred Practice

The childish work for their own benefit
The Buddhas work for the benefit of others
Just look at the difference between them!

You will find, as I have, that if you make the practice of Tonglen your own, you will experience the depths of your own compassion and innate generosity. You will come to realize that far from being too fragile to bear the pain of the world—one of the most effective fictions of the false self—you are in fact far better able than you ever imagined to confront what is really happening in the world, and far more powerful an agent of healing than you ever suspected.

Before you begin to do the practice of Tonglen itself, I advise you to follow the Tibetan mystics' advice and sit for five or ten minutes in calm silence. The calmer and more inwardly peaceful you are, the stronger you will feel when it comes to confronting your own or others' suffering.

I find it very powerful at the beginning of Tonglen practice to imagine that I am staring out across a still and sunlit ocean or up into the boundless blue depths of a spring sky. Doing this, I find, immediately expands my mind and makes it more spacious. I also find it helpful to pray to all those awakened beings, such as Jesus, Rumi, and the Buddha, who have made the practice of compassion the core of their message: I pray to them all to come and help me claim, live, and enact the truth of the Divine Compassion within me and within all beings.

Now, with mind and heart composed, begin the practice of giving and taking by doing Tonglen on yourself. One highly effective way of doing this is to practice seated before a large mirror in which you can see yourself clearly. Let the person in the mirror—let's call him or her A—be your biological self, with all its sadness, doubts, fears, and difficulties; let the person gazing into the mirror—B—be your eternal self already free, already liberated, whose essence is spacious and all-embracing love.

Gaze now with the eyes of your eternal free self at what I call "the wreck in the mirror." Gaze without fear or shame and see clearly in A's face all of A's loneliness, worry, panic, and grief. Note everything calmly, compassionately, and without judgment. Remind yourself that the biological self is the *reflection,* in the mirror of life, of a far more powerful and spacious *eternal self* who cannot be destroyed or broken. Allow the beauty of this knowledge to infuse your whole being with joy and faith.

Now imagine that all the fears and desolations your biological self is harboring issue from the stomach of your image in the mirror in the form of a ball of hot, black, grimy smoke. Clearly visualize this ball of thickly swirling black smoke. Then, as you breathe in, breathe the black ball into the fully open heart center of your eternal self and imagine it dissolving away completely there, as smoke would in a cloudless shining blue sky. Then, on the out-breath, breathe back at your biological self in the mirror all your eternal self's peace, bliss, strength, and healing power.

Make sure that your in-breaths and out-breaths are equally deep and long. Breathe in the black ball of smoke from the stomach of your biological self; pause and imagine it dissolving in the boundless blue sky of your eternal heart-mind. Then breathe out as deeply and fully as you breathed in, consciously sending out to your biological self as you do so all you know of the faith and radiance of your own divine truth.

If you do this nine times calmly and confidently, you will be amazed at how much better and more grounded you will feel. You will now be ready to turn to the second part of the practice.

In this second part of Tonglen, you will be giving and receiving for someone else. Select a person who you know is in psychological or physical pain. Imagine him or her clearly in your heart's eye; meditate as deeply and sensitively as you can on all the difficulties he or she is experiencing and all the grief and fear he or she must be feeling. If the person you have chosen is someone you have had conflicts with, or someone you have ambiguous feelings for, don't be surprised if these surface and try to block your compassion toward him. When these feelings arise, offer them for transformation. You can even, as I often do, perform a kind of mini-Tonglen on the feelings themselves: breathe the difficult feelings in, then breathe out to yourself the compassion of your innate nature.

Now imagine that all the psychological or physical anguish of the person you have chosen issues from her stomach in the concentrated form of a hot, black, grimy ball of smoke. As you breathe in, breathe in that black ball of hot smoke; as you breathe out, breathe out to her all the peace, strength, happiness, and bliss of your innate love nature.

Something a young Tibetan practitioner once told me has helped me immensely in this stage of the practice. He said, "Never be afraid that if you breathe in someone's pain that it will some-how 'get stuck' in you. Remember that there is nowhere in you for it to get stuck; in your essence, you are the boundless space of Buddha consciousness." Reminding myself of what he told me has prevented me time and time again from involuntarily closing down to the being I have chosen to practice for. He also told me to imagine that as I breathe out, the blessing my out-breath sends to the person I have chosen doesn't end with him or her but travels on and on throughout the universe. "All acts of true compassion," he said, "are infinite both in their origin and in their effect. Imagine that your out-breath cleanses, purifies, and blesses not only the person you have chosen, but the whole cosmos." As you breathe out, then, imagine with great faith that the person you have chosen is completely irradiated with grace and healed of everything that afflicts her. It helps to see, in your heart's eye, the person smiling or laughing or dancing with joy and health. Imagine that the blessing of her joy and health is contagious and spreads invisibly through all things everywhere, illumining them all with Divine Light.

Now, in the third part of the practice, turn in your heart to confront the suffering of the whole planet. Imagine the birds and mammals dying in forest fires, the sea creatures suffering from pollution, the women and children murdered or maimed in wars, the monotonous horror of the lives of the desperately poor in slums and ghettos. Imagine the danger the planet faces from environmental destruction of all kinds and from the possibility of nuclear annihilation. With all the force of the Divine within you, try to face, without illusion or false consolation, all the aspects of the agony that the entire planet is now going through.

Imagine now that the entire earth is a ball of hot, black, grimy smoke in which all these horrors are concentrated. Imagine, too, that the Divine Self you are now is as vast as the universe. Take that vast black ball of agony into your heart and dissolve it in your heart's pure transparence. Breathe in the earth's black smoke; pause as it dissolves utterly in your sky-like heart, breathe out the light and bliss and strength of your Divine Self and imagine the whole earth bathed in its healing glory. Do this nine times slowly, with total concentration.

Your intention to transmute the suffering of all sentient beings and of the whole earth has transformed you now into a diamond being whose body, heart, mind, and spirit are on fire with brilliant white Divine Light. Send this light with its all-transforming powers in all the four directions, and know with faith and joy that it will do wonders and instigate great secret healings.

As you keep sending out the brilliant white light from your diamond body, make a vow to renew your Sacred Activism with devotion and humility.

A Prayer Practice: The Prayer of Saint Francis

I recommend that all Sacred Activists recite and meditate on the Prayer of Saint Francis.

When I was 18, I spent eight months hitchhiking around Italy. At the time, I was about to go to Oxford, and I thought that I wanted to be an art historian. So I visited all the great centers—Florence, Rome, Naples, and Venice. Then, one day in early May, I found myself in Assisi, where Saint Francis had lived and died. Nothing I had seen prepared me for the impact of Giotto's paintings of the life of Saint Francis in the basilica; their grave, exalted purity dazzled me. I decided to stay to contemplate them for a week, and I slept out in the ruins of an old castle, surrounded by the rough, fragrant hills of Tuscany in spring.

I can still remember the sunlit afternoon when, sitting in a field of yellow and blue wildflowers, I first read the Prayer of Saint

Francis. Every word pierced me with the freshness of Giotto's vision and of that high and noble Tuscan landscape:

> Lord, make me an instrument of thy peace.
> Where there is hatred, let me sow love;
> Where there is injury, pardon;
> Where there is doubt, faith;
> Where there is despair, hope;
> Where there is darkness, light;
> Where there is sadness, joy.
>
> O Divine Master, grant that I may not so much seek
> To be consoled as to console,
> To be understood as to understand,
> To be loved as to love:
> For it is in giving that we receive,
> It is in pardoning that we are pardoned,
> It is in dying that we are born to eternal life.

I remember that afternoon, reading the prayer over and over, savoring every word, how astonished I was at its spiritual truth and beauty. The more I contemplated the prayer and the holy passions behind it, the deeper my joy became, until I, the sunlit afternoon, and the wind moving in the brilliant flowers seemed to become one vast sustained movement of adoration within the being of God.

The practice I am going to describe is found in its essential outlines in many of the mystical traditions; it has great power to transform your heart and personality.

Memorize the Saint Francis Prayer. Then, sitting calmly in meditation, say it over and over again to yourself very slowly, bringing your mind home to its words whenever it begins to stray. Do this for about half an hour at a time and you will find that your mind and heart will be made joyful and peaceful and that, over time, your entire being will begin to fill with the strengths and virtues that the passage celebrates. All mystical systems know that we become what we think; this exercise is a wonderful way of saturating the heart and mind with holy truth and passion.

That afternoon in Tuscany 40 years ago initiated me into the prayer's mystic power, and everything I have learned since on my search has only deepened my joy at its depth. It seems to me a prayer that transcends any particular religion; in a very few utterly stripped and simple phrases, it condenses the deepest wisdom of the Path of Sacred Activism. Over the years I have shared it with seekers and activists of all kinds; they have all recognized the transmuting power of the holy inspiration that still sings in its lines. One young Tibetan doctor I met in Ladakh translated it into Tibetan and started to use it every day in his morning prayers to the Buddha of Compassion. A Hindu devotee of Shiva I know, who works with slum children in Mumbai, uses it every morning in her prayers to the "Lord of Love."

Begin by sitting calmly in your place of meditation, breathing in and out deeply to steady your mind. If you have any incense, light a stick of it so the whole atmosphere around you can become fragrant.

When you feel ready, read the entire prayer slowly once through, savoring each word and trying to enter as deeply as you can into the meaning of each phrase. When you have done so, rest a little in the sacred emotion such a reading will arouse.

I find it helpful at this moment to pray to God to open me still more deeply to the holy passion of the prayer. Often I say something like "May the love speaking this prayer open me completely to itself!" or "Remove all fear from my mind and heart so it can go fearlessly into the fire of absolute love!"

Then, slowly, I start to say inwardly the first line: "Lord, make me an instrument of thy peace." I try to dwell richly on each phrase. What does it mean to say "Lord, *make* me," for example? What *is* an instrument of peace, and what has to be given up in oneself to become one? Why does Saint Francis seem to stress the holiness of peace above all other aspects of the spiritual life? What is thy peace? To each inner question I try to bring the totality of everything that I have understood about these questions from my search and from my own experience and from the experience of others.

Very often my mind starts to wander almost immediately. Something about the power and beauty of this prayer scares it profoundly. I think this is a prayer that breathes in each phrase the kind of sacred selflessness that terrifies the ego. I try to be compassionate to my mind and its need to evade the seriousness of the prayer's intentions, but I also try not to let it wander too far. As soon as I catch it wandering, I bring it back to the line of the prayer it was contemplating before it started to wander. This can be difficult work, but it is worth it. It trains the attention and, over time, allows the sacred power of the prayer to infuse the mind and spirit at profound levels.

Slowly and with as much sacred concentration as I can muster, I go through the prayer phrase by phrase, trying to bring everything I know and long for to my reading of it. Then, after a brief pause, I go back to the beginning. In the course of half an hour's meditation, it is rare that I find myself saying the prayer in this way more than 12 or 13 times; instead, I find that if I practice with sufficient devotion and sincerity, the prayer draws me into the passionate silence of the heart that it was created from. To enter and become one with this silence is the true goal of all prayer. So, when this silence arrives, I stop speaking the words of the prayer inwardly and continue only when my mind starts getting restive.

At the end of the practice, I find it helpful to recite the entire prayer once more, steadily and slowly, dedicating my whole being to its force and power. Then, as the final act of the exercise, I dedicate whatever insights and sacred emotions saying the prayer has aroused in me to the awakening of all sentient beings. To make this dedication at the end more real and vivid, I imagine that saying it sends dazzling white light in all directions in God's name, light that will heal, save, inspire, and embolden all those it invisibly touches.

A Sacred Body Practice: Savasana

I would like to share a restorative practice from the Heart Yoga that Karuna Erickson and I developed. The following excerpt from our book *On Fire: Heart Yoga* describes one of the simplest but most transformative of yoga positions, Savasana, a position I use several times a day (especially when working hard) to bring my body into sacred alignment.

> Lie down on your back with your arms stretched out. Begin with your knees bent, feet flat on the floor. Gradually draw your awareness inward. Consciously and slowly, one at a time, lengthen your heels out along the floor, inviting your legs to fall back and rest.
>
> Elongate your arms down to your sides, releasing any last vestige of stress or exhaustion. Turn your palms up into a soft, receptive position, like a baby's hands. Feel yourself letting go of whatever you have been holding on to.
>
> Allow the skin of your face to soften away from the bones. Your eyes drop back in their sockets, away from the inside of your eyelids. The gaze moves down, resting in the warmth of the heart. Vision now seems to come from your heart. Your ears also turn inward towards the heart, to listen to its whispering.
>
> As you drop deeper and deeper into Savasana, your skin starts to grow more porous and transparent, almost translucent, so that the light inside you can radiate outwards and the light all around you pours inwards. As your skin continues to open to the light, your boundaries begin to soften and dissolve.
>
> The boundaries of your personality also begin to soften. Let go now of anything that keeps you separate from other beings and from the joy and bliss of your essential nature, letting it all float away like clouds in an infinite blue sky.
>
> From this vast awareness, find your breath and follow its path as it flows down into your body with your

inhalation and as it empties out with your exhalation. Breathing in, your eyes soften; exhaling, your breath dissolves into emptiness. Breathe down into earth, breathe out into spaciousness.

Notice the moments of stillness at the very end of the inhalation and at the very completion of the exhalation. This is not a holding, but rather a suspension of your breath. Imagine this pause like a hawk suspended on a current of air. With the inhalation, drop down deep into the still pool of the pause at its end. Follow the exhalation all the way to its completion, and savor the exquisite moment at the end when it dissolves into space, like smoke disappearing into the sky. Inhale, and pause for a few heartbeats; exhale, and pause for a few heartbeats. Continue this practice for a few minutes.

Breathe into stillness and breathe out into spaciousness, returning again and again to the breath, to the breath inside the breath. Breathe into the earth, the Mother; breathe out to the sky, the Father. Offer your body, mind, and heart onto the altar of service. Expand and dissolve into the spaciousness of Savasana.

Let the spaciousness of the silence soak into every pore of your skin and every cell of your body. Let the silence take you to the core of your life. Rest in Savasana at least ten minutes.

When you feel ready to return from the spaciousness of Savasana, very slowly bring your awareness to your breath. Visualize your breath as a mist drifting toward you across a vast snowy field. Watch it flow into the core of your body, gently and tenderly touching the deepest places inside you. Feel each inhalation as a blessing and each exhalation as a prayer. Remember that this peace and stillness are always available to you, in any circumstances, simply by returning your awareness to your breath.

Grounded in this awareness, slowly begin your journey back from Savasana. Rise back up from Savasana gradually, like a deep-sea diver slowly returning from the depths of the sea. Pause when you want to pause. Remain connected to the beauty you experienced in the oceanic depths of yourself.

Let your transition back from Savasana be gentle, gradually coming fully into your body. Feel the warmth and radiance that surround your body and the touch of the air on your face. Listen to the sounds around you.

When you are fully present in your body, in this moment and this breath, roll to your right side, feeling the support of the earth beneath you. Slowly let your eyelids part, keeping your eyes soft, your brain quiet, and your heart open.

Let your soft, compassionate presence radiate out from you. Imagine it cradling the whole world, and offer the benefits of your practice for the peace and liberation of all sentient beings. When you feel ready, sit up, and bring your hands to the Namaste position in front of your heart.

Bow to all beings and dedicate your life to their sacred service.

CHAPTER 10

THE LAW OF SURRENDERING THE FRUITS OF ACTION TO THE DIVINE

Mark Dubois, co-founder of the International Rivers network, risked his life in 1979 to protect a wild canyon from being flooded in conjunction with the damming of the Stanislaus River in Northern California. He chained himself to a rock in the canyon and so succeeded in preventing the flood. As he chained himself to the rock, Mark had an epiphany. "When I was in the canyon it didn't matter what the outcome was. It was the most liberating sensation I ever had. I felt very powerful. I found my voice completely, and I was speaking out from my deep truth. I was laying my life on the line for something I believed in with all my heart."

What Mark Dubois discovered in the canyon was the joy, peace, inner certainty, and freedom that come to you when you perform action not from your own private agenda, but as a prayer on behalf of all life and as a sacrifice of love offered to God. All the mystical traditions tell us that for action to be the sacred channel of Divine Grace, it needs to be performed selflessly and for the sake of God alone. As Saint Paul writes in I Corinthians 30-31, "Whether therefore ye eat or drink, or whatsoever ye do, do all to the glory of God."

Performing action in this way makes it holy. It also protects the doer from dangerous illusory belief in his or her own personal agency and from the karma that accrues to actions performed out of ignorance, passion, or desire. The sages of Hinduism and Buddhism tell us that when action is grounded in a spirit of compassionate service to sentient beings and to God, it does not accrue karma. They tell us that because the doer has surrendered the fruits of action (given up all results of action to the divine will) and has purified her inner being of anything but a desire to serve others and serve God, she experiences herself as the instrument of divine will, and, knowing herself surrendered, knows in the middle of action a peace, bliss, and strength that the storms of the world cannot destroy.

Perhaps the most profound instruction on the necessity of surrendering the fruit of action is given by Krishna to Arjuna in the great Hindu scripture the Bhagavad Gita. Prince Arjuna stands desolate and disconsolate on the eve of a great battle against his own kinsmen, the Pandavas. Arjuna is full of grief and doubt about the best course of action. His charioteer, Krishna, reveals himself as the Divine and instructs the Prince in the truth of Karma Yoga— the way to God through action dedicated to the Divine, the way of Sacred Activism: "Great is the man, who, free from attachments and with a mind ruling its powers in harmony, works on the path of Karma Yoga, the path of consecrated action."

Krishna continues:

"Action is greater than inaction. Perform thy task in life. Even the life of the body could not be if there were no action.

"The world is in the bonds of action, unless the action is consecration. Let thy actions then be pure, free from the bonds of desire . . .

"The man who has found the joy of the spirit and in the spirit has satisfaction, who in the spirit has found his peace, that man is beyond the law of action.

"In liberty from the bonds of attachment, do thou therefore the work to be done, for the man whose work is pure attains indeed the Supreme."

In acting in this selfless way, Krishna tells Arjuna, the human being attains the Supreme. This is because action performed in this way mirrors the working of the Divine itself. God works out of pure love, with no need for any result or reward. As Krishna says: "I have no work at all to do in all the worlds, Arjuna—for these are mine. I have nothing to obtain, for I have all. And yet I work. If ever my work had an end, these worlds would end in destruction and confusion would reign . . ."

Krishna continues:

"Even as the unwise work selfishly in the bondage of selfish works, let the wise man work unselfishly for the good of all the world.

"Offer to me all the works and rest thy mind on the Supreme. Be free from vain hopes and selfish thoughts, and with inner peace fight thou thy fight.

"Be one in self-harmony, in Yoga, and arise, great warrior, arise."

Illumined by sacred wisdom, Arjuna goes into battle, offering himself and all his doubts and desires up to God. In God's name and for God's glory, Arjuna wins the battle and, acting as God's humble instrument, rights his world.

The Bhagavad Gita gives us the highest and most exalted instruction possible on the nature of sacred action as an act of selfless sacrifice to the Supreme. When you try to put this sacred teaching into practice in the world, you discover that it is as practical as it is exalted. You discover that there are three reasons why all the mystical traditions stress this law of surrender as essential to the working out of the divine will in the world in Sacred Activism.

The first reason is that it is only by becoming as selfless in your motives and as surrendered in your being as possible that you can hope to follow divine guidance and so begin to know what the will of the Divine expects, wants, and demands of you. If your being is full of your own plans and your mind and heart noisy and turbulent with your own projects and desires, the mysterious and sometimes strange and paradoxical instructions of God cannot illumine you to bring your sacred work to fruition. Divine guidance is always available, but only the surrendered receive it in its clear, pure form.

The second reason why the Gita's teaching is practical is that only by surrendering the fruits of action to the Divine can you perform your actions with a calmness and humility that will protect you from despair and keep you secretly fed from your deepest divine sources. Nothing could be more important for all of us to learn than this Law—that it is only by giving up the results of what you do to God that you can rescue yourself from the distress, anxiety, and harassing anguish that inevitably accompany real work in the real world when it is done from a personal agenda. The more important the work, the more you need a serene inner detachment from its outcome; otherwise, knowing how vital it is will crucify you with anxiety and drive you to despair or even self-loathing when you feel you have failed in the mission entrusted to you.

The teaching of the Gita is practical for a third reason: only surrendering the fruits of action to the Divine can help the Sacred Activist cultivate the patience he will need. Patience is for me, and for many with a passionate nature and a sense of outrage, the hardest of all virtues to acquire—but for real work in a real world that often changes slowly, painfully, and ambiguously, patience is essential.

Gandhi worked for over 40 years, often against nearly impossible odds, to free India from the British. Martin Luther King, Jr., dedicated his entire life to the victory of civil rights and died before he could see the Promised Land; many of my environmental activist friends have been hunkered down for almost 30 years in poorly paid positions and only now feel that the world might be starting to listen to them. Hardly any of the major breakthroughs in world history have come quickly, and the Sacred Activists who struggle for them have not only had to accept the obstinacy, brutality, and hard-headedness of the powers ranged against them, but also had to forge in their souls the kind of patience that enables them to keep working steadily for their goal even when its realization seems unattainable. Without this patience as the bedrock of sacred action, the fullness of the divine blessing cannot mature in and through it. As Allah says in the Koran, "God is with the patient."

CHAPTER 11

THE LAW OF
RECOGNIZING EVIL

It is time for all Sacred Activists to stop being naïve about the power of the destructive forces both within themselves and in the world. In the great battle that we have come to for the future of the human race, it would be dangerous not to be as aware as possible of the potential for destructiveness in yourself and aware, too, of the enormous power for harm that these forces have in the real world. Only this kind of realism can prepare you for what you have to face; only this kind of realism will give you adequate protection as you set about doing your sacred work.

The great mystical systems are realistic about the presence and power of evil. They know that evil plays a necessary role in our reality that must be recognized and respected. Sacred Activists cannot afford to be naïve about their own shadows, about the shadow sides of the political, religious, economic, and religious establishments, or about what Saint Paul called "the powers and principalities"—occult destructive forces that are part of the One and that wreak havoc if we do not acknowledge their strength and make every wise effort made to protect ourselves against them, inwardly and outwardly.

In the early '90s I was at a meeting in New York with several of the leading organizers of what was to be the U.N. Conference on Environment and Development in Rio. A quiet, handsome, well-dressed man in his 40s took me aside afterward and introduced himself as the head of a major agribusiness corporation. He said, "I have something very important to tell you, and I will pay for the joy of telling it to you by offering you lunch."

At lunch the next day, he cut to the chase: "Rio will accomplish absolutely nothing because you do-gooders are so naïve about the real world. Most of you that I have met truly believe that if the CEOs—like me, for instance—*really* knew what harm their corporate policies were doing, they would rend their Armani suits, fling out their Rolex-wreathed arms, burst into tears, and change. This is madness and shows how little you dare to know about what is really going on. And how can you even begin to be effective until you understand what you are up against?

"Let me tell you what you are up against. You are up against people like me. I know exactly what my company is doing and what devastation it is causing to thousands of lives. I should know; I am running it. I know and I do not care. I have decided I want a grand gold-plated lifestyle and the perks and jets and houses that go with it and I will do anything—bend the law, have people 'removed,' bribe local governmental officials, you name it—to get what I want. I know, too, that none of my shareholders care a rat's ass what I do or how I do it, providing I keep them swimming in cash.

"I said that you were up against people like me. That is true in one sense, but not in another. Because the truth is that I am in you too. A part of you is like me, just as ruthless and dedicated to your own selfish agenda. But you can dress up this ruthlessness as your 'mission' and never unmask the lust for power that might be lurking behind your righteous facade.

"What limits all so-called seekers and activists that I meet is that they both shy away from the full realization of the power of the dark. The seekers I meet are, frankly, 'bliss bunnies,' about as useful in the real world as a rubber ball would be in a war. The activists I know enjoy denouncing others but aren't at all in the business of unmasking their own destructiveness, or the self-destructiveness of their dreary and banal self-righteousness.

"The bliss-bunnyhood of seekers and the offensive self-righteousness of activists make it very easy for people like me to control the world. I know too, by the way, that the dark forces I play with are playing with me. I am under no illusion that I will not someday have to pay the price. Don't the French say, 'The devil has no friends'? I'm willing to pay that price in return for the pleasure of being able to afford this restaurant, in return for being able to ring up the president of the United States in front of house-guests to impress them. Am I getting through to you?"

"You are," I said. "Thank you. You have taught me a lesson today that I will try to remember even when I don't want to." Although I heard clearly what he said and the way he said it, with the cynical bravura of someone who thought himself massively smarter than anyone else, I could also hear dark wisdom in what he was trying to tell me, and I knew I *needed* to hear it, and that he was, in a perverse way, may well have been trying to give me a gift.

The well-meaning if self-serving naïveté of my nature had already exposed me to much suffering, and I knew that any work in the world that I would want to do would have to be born as much out of what Jesus called "the wisdom of the serpent" as out of "the innocence of the dove." In this man I met the dark personal hunger for power that has seductive allure in all realms, including the so-called spiritual. When I left my guru, I met, in the course of my own prolonged Dark Night, the forces of *impersonal* evil; what Saint Paul calls "the powers and principalities," the dark cosmic forces that are also at work in the world and universe. I have described this encounter at length in my book *Sun at Midnight:* one of the characteristics of the Dark Night known in the mystical systems is that in it you lose all illusions about human nature, including your own, and meet, in a way that shocks you to your core, the unmasked ferocious forces of the occult that menace your external and inner life, in sometimes near-lethal ways. I myself was especially vulnerable because I had no knowledge of these occult forces; I had to wake up fast and learn how to protect myself to stay alive.

My vision of Sacred Activism has been partly forged out of these "encounters" with the dark without and within, and I am grateful for the sobering wisdom they gave me. If I had not set out after my meeting with the agribusiness tycoon to understand what he had told me about himself and the world of power he was speaking for, I would still be under the illusion that something less than a total divine transformation of human nature could preserve us from the danger we are in. If I hadn't met, in a undeniable way, the power of the impersonal occult forces ranged against any evolutionary progress (which are well known in all authentic mystical systems), I would imagine that being on the side of the "good" and "doing one's best" would be enough. It is not enough.

Only constant spiritual practice can deepen your realization of essential unity with the One so that you can begin to face, from the strength and joy that realization gives you, the darkness you must confront in yourself and in the dynamics of the world. It is only by realizing the One Consciousness in its essential aspect of transcendent bliss and peace within yourself that you can begin to face the ferocity of its alchemical dance of good and evil, light and dark, in reality. Unless you face this ferocity without fear or illusion or denial, you cannot work effectively for change in a time like ours.

If, as I believe, the vision of Sacred Activism I have presented can create the crucible for the birth of the Divine Human, then both the destructive forces within the world and the impersonal occult forces have every reason to try to stop the full unleashing of its power. After all, mystics who leave the world to its own devices while soaring off into their own transcendent trance do not threaten any of the world's hierarchies or elites, and activists who work from a divided consciousness burn out easily, are easily manipulated, and are rarely, for all their righteous intentions, conscious channels for the power of Divine Grace.

The Sacred Activist, however, who fuses profound mystical knowledge, stamina, peace, and passion with wise, focused action in the world is the most dangerous of all beings to those destructive forces that long to undo the human experiment. Being dangerous, the Sacred Activist will be in danger if he doesn't know how to stay alert to its signs, prepared for the difficulties and obstacles the forces of dark power will try to create, and awake to the forces within him that invite the dark and give it room to work.

Nothing of what I am saying here would be foreign to the sages who created the I Ching, or to great Mahayana mystics, or to Rumi, or to the great Christian masters of the Dark Night, such as Teresa of Avila and Saint John of the Cross. But part of the terrible price we have paid for our addiction to reason and our dismissal of mystical reality is total ignorance of these destructive forces—not only of their nature, but of their very existence—which gives them even greater power.

What has given me hope in my journey into recognition of these forces is the wisdom of protection the mystical traditions offer. This wisdom of protection is, as usual, perfectly summed up by Rumi:

> The Prophet said, "Prudence consists of staring evil
> in the face."
> Know, you madman, each of your steps is a trap.
> The surface of the plain seems smooth and vast.
> But there's a trap at every step.
> Don't go forward arrogantly.
> The mountain goat skips along saying,
> "I don't see any trap!"
> While it races, the snare pierces its throat.
> You who say, "Where is this trap?"
> Look and gaze around you, and know
> You've seen the plain but not the trap . . .
> If you have eyes, don't walk blindly
> And if you haven't, take a cane with you.
> If you don't have the cane of prudence and judgment,
> Take the eyes of one who sees as guide.
> When you proceed, proceed like a blind man, so your feet
> Avoid the ditch and the wild dogs.
> The blind man makes his way trembling with fear,

Taking every precaution to avoid all nuisance.
If you don't act like him, you fool,
You'll have leapt far from the smoke
Only to fall headlong into the fire.

The greatest protection, as Rumi makes clear, is the real, sober-ing knowledge of the traps that are set for the naïve and arrogant. Having the courage to acquire this sometimes bitter wisdom leads in time to the real, saving knowledge—which Rumi also makes clear—that in doing sacred work your greatest protections are continual and radical humility, ever more astute discrimination, and a canny prudence. Otherwise, for all your noble intentions and compassionate motivations, your work will be wrecked on the rocks of reality.

The great challenge for the Sacred Activist is to acquire this humility, discrimination, and prudence without becoming afraid or cynical; to combine, in other words, faith in the mercy of the One with fearless and unillusioned knowledge of the One's alchemy in reality. This alchemy is a marriage of opposites, inac-cessible to reason, that is perfectly creative only in the enlight-ened; the rest of us have to constantly strive for it in a deeper and deeper commitment to see the world and reality as they really are and not what any human fantasy, however well-intentioned, would want them to be.

THREE PRACTICES OF PROTECTION AGAINST EVIL

There are three powerful protection practices that I often use. The first I was taught, in the aftermath of my leaving my guru, by a clairvoyant healer who was a disciple of Padre Pio. The second I evolved myself though hard work with my Jungian analyst. The third I discovered, with growing wonder and delight, for myself.

Turn to the Divine Mother

Turn to the Divine Mother in whatever way you imagine her. Put yourself constantly under her direct protection, the protection of the Mother of the universe. I use a simple Eastern Orthodox prayer: "Mother, save me, protect me, heal me, illumine me, light up with your Eternal Light the dangers around me and in me, and give me the wisdom and faith I need." Once you have placed yourself, in whatever way is natural to you, under the protection of the Motherhood of God, then imagine that you are completely surrounded with pink light. The great healer who taught me this told me that the power of this pink light—the Light of Divine Love given off by the Eternal Rose of the Eternal Feminine—has been known by esoteric healers in Europe for centuries. Because of its purity of Love, it has ultimate power against the evil.

Listen to Your Dreams

This second practice invites you to listen to the messages your unconscious can send in dreams. Whenever I am involved in a demanding project in the world and have come to a difficult threshold or want to know how to proceed with what I am doing, I make a point, before going to sleep, of asking my unconscious to give me instruction in a way I can understand. As you learn *how* to listen to your unconscious, you gain greater and greater access to your hidden powers of clairvoyance and discrimination. At first, you may need the skillful help of someone practiced in dream work, such as I received from my Jungian analyst, to tap into the guidance of your unconscious in this way. But soon you will find that if you pray before falling asleep to be instructed as unambiguously and clearly as possible, in time you will be. The confidence in your own deep resources that will build from this growing encounter with your unconscious will give you greater faith in yourself and help you correct your course when you need to. You will also learn that if you don't listen to the warnings that come, thinking your conscious mind knows better, you will put yourself in danger.

Consult and Respect the I Ching

Twenty years ago, a friend gave me Richard Wilhelm's translation of the I Ching, the great ancient Chinese book known as the Book of Changes. He told me that the I Ching had been consulted throughout Chinese history by people in every stratum of society. Then, with great reverence, he taught me how to approach it with a question and, by throwing coins, find a hexagram that gives an answer and so gave me one of the holiest and most helpful gifts I have ever received.

This is not the place to go into the complex theory of the 64 hexagrams of the I Ching or the reasons why a respectful consultation of it always, in my long experience, yields startlingly wise guidance. Suffice it to say that I strongly advise all those wanting to become Sacred Activists to avail themselves of this most realistic and subtle of ancient oracles.

You will find that if you take the trouble to study the I Ching in some depth and to develop a relationship of profound respect with it, it will repay your reverence and sincerity by offering you advice that will provide the most precise and powerful protection for you in everything you do. The two versions I recommend are the Richard Wilhelm translation, with a masterly introduction by Carl Jung, and *The Complete I Ching,* the definitive translation by Taoist master Alfred Huang, a masterpiece of scholarship and mystical wisdom that combines a shrewd grasp of modern life with a comprehensive knowledge of Chinese tradition.

CHAPTER 12

THE LAW OF
THE ALCHEMY
OF ANGER

For the Sacred Activist, the problem of anger represents one of the deepest spiritual challenges. On the one hand, as everyone has experienced, anger can blind your judgment and lead you into folly, hatred, and a furious and brutal self-righteousness that immediately repels those you hope to persuade or inspire. On the other, when alchemized by deep spiritual insight in the container of spiritual practice, anger can provide the fuel for working in the world with the laser-like energy of fierce compassion and wisdom.

If you and I are not outraged by what is happening everywhere in our world, we will remain where so many find themselves, in paralysis, apathy and denial. Yet if our outrage masters us, we may become irrational, violent, and destructive in our turn, inwardly ravaged by rage at, and hatred of our opponents that will not only dehumanize us but also cripple our effectiveness.

If we work with this anger and outrage, however, without repressing or judging or denying it, within the crucible of spiritual practice, it can be transformed into a reservoir of purified passion, compassion and wisdom that will give us power and stamina. Julia Butterfly Hill has described this process in an interview with Andrew Beath in *Consciousness in Action:*

In today's world, it's not only our right to be angry, it's our responsibility. The question is, do we act out of anger or love? That's what makes the difference. The reason I feel it's our responsibility to be angry is that anyone who looks at the world will recognize that we hurt innocent life, and bring more children into the world who will be injured. The anger comes from knowing we have the potential to do it another way and yet we don't. Then we let go, and the anger becomes secondary. I do what I do because of my love, not my anger.

My prayer is that I may be an open heart. When I become angry at what we're doing, I take it in and say, "Okay, anger through love becomes fierce compassion." Anger is a powerful energy and I'm all for using energy, whatever form it comes in, but using it for the good. When I first got stressed out in the tree, I'd take a deep breath in and say, "Stress in and stress out." I don't want to lose the passion of anger. It's a vital life force. Later I changed the practice and said, "Stress in, love out" with each breath . . . I still have passion, but I can look at someone who threatens to kill me, and my heart melts. I see their injury makes them act that way. It helps me transform difficult situations.

I have often used the practice Julia Butterfly Hill gives here to help transmute the outrage I feel at cruelty, injustice, and denial into a purified passion of compassion that can fuel steady work for change. I know by now that the deepest source of my energy, and my best quality as a teacher and writer, is the passion I bring to what I do; it is this passion that has given me the hunger and energy to evolve on my path, and I have resisted any attempts to muffle or repress it. I also know that the shadow of this passion is anger, cruelty, and a ferociously judgmental arrogance that has sometimes made me ineffective, unforgiving, ungenerous, isolated, and despairing. My challenge has been not to repress this passion but to recognize it as sacred, while also working constantly on purifying and refining it so that it does not become an enemy to me or to others.

A PRACTICE OF TRANSMUTING ANGER
IN THE PRESENCE OF THE DARK FEMININE

I have found that the best and most effective way to transmute outrage into fierce, compassionate wisdom energy is to work with the Force that is itself both loving and fierce, tender and ferocious: the Mother in her dark aspect as Kali or the Black Madonna. I know that the sacred roots of my outrage are in Her passionate and protective love for all beings and for the creation. I know also that while this fierce love is pure and married to ultimate wisdom in Her being, it is muddied by exaggeration, hysteria, childhood trauma, and impatience in mine.

I imagine the Black Madonna or Kali standing in front of me, majestic and radiating golden light. From my open heart center I send toward her heart a stream of golden flame intermingled with acrid black smoke. The golden flame is the part of my outrage that is sacred and inspired by Her wild love for all beings and for justice. The acrid black smoke represents the part of my outrage that is conditioned by human panic, rage, and neurosis. I pray to Her: "Mother, take this golden flame of sacred passion, inter-twined with the black smoke of my neurosis and trauma, into the depths of Your heart. So transmute it there in You that You can return it to me in a stream of pure golden love-fire that has had all the darkness removed from it." Then I visualize the stream of golden fire mixed with acrid black smoke streaming from my open heart center to Hers. I visualize Her heart center opening to receive it, closing to transmute it, and opening again to send me back a stream of pure golden passion-energy, a passion-energy that has been purified in Her and by Her.

I take this pure golden passion-energy into my heart center and imagine it traveling up to the top of my head and down to the ends of my toes, suffusing my mind, heart, and body with its brilliant power. At the end of the practice, I imagine myself prostrating before Kali or the Black Madonna and praying, "Keep me always in this growing balance between fierceness and tenderness, judgment and compassion, and fill me always through Your grace with this golden, purified passionate energy of wisdom and love."

I have found this to be a powerful practice, especially in difficult and dangerous situations where the energy that outrage and passion can give is essential, but where its unguarded, unwise, or violent expression would be disastrous. In a world such as ours, such situations are all too frequent.

CHAPTER 13

THE LAW OF CONSTANT, HUMBLE SHADOW WORK

Carl Jung wrote in *Psychology and Alchemy,* "The shadow personifies everything that the subject refuses to acknowledge about himself and yet is always thrusting itself upon him directly or indirectly." He adds, "The shadow does not consist of small weaknesses and blemishes, but of a truly demonic dynamic." Jung did not use the word *demonic* for effect. He used the word *demonic* because it is through our shadow that the destructive forces that are part of the alchemically creative nature of the One wreak their havoc, violence, suffering, and destruction.

It must be clear by now that I see the Death we are living through as the masterpiece of our communal and communally unacknowledged shadow. The false self in its increasingly crazed addiction to domination over nature is engineering its own suicide. All the ruling powers of our world cast dangerous shadows— political shadows of corrupt manipulation, religious shadows of authoritarian control in the various hierarchies of the religions and guru systems, and corporate shadows of heartless exploitation. Every profession and vocation, including that of spiritual teacher, is now perverted by a world whose fundamental values have largely become success for its own sake, status, and fame. The shadow of brutal greed is cast by the collective false self across all the realms in which it operates, with the inner and outer results we are now enduring.

Seeing this takes courage, and seeing it as a "demonic dynamic" poised to destroy everything we hold dear takes even more courage. What takes the deepest courage, in my experience, however, is to face in yourself that same demonic dynamic without mask or illusion, both in your own personal shadow, formed from humiliation, fear of death, and the drive to power, and in the ways that it links up with and feeds the demonic dynamic of the collective shadow.

In authentic shadow work, you will be compelled to discover that everything you hate in others lives in you—that everything you fear in the destructive forces raging in our world has a home in you in some dark corner, in an unacknowledged unhealed fear or trauma, a hunger to be unique and special, or an unexamined desire for revenge.

No one wants to do this work or face these scalding insights. I began a serious journey into the shadow two years ago after the end of my marriage because I wanted to understand my own part in that wreck and I knew that there must be much I was refusing to acknowledge about myself. I also knew that my evolution of Sacred Activism had reached an impasse—the impasse of my own disbelief in the power of my own vision, which led me to present it in public too vehemently and aggressively. I knew there must be a connection between these two harsh koans, but I also knew that I could not see it on my own. I knew that if my marriage had ended so darkly and my work was suffering from what I experienced as a kind of inner split, there must be recognition within me of my own hidden addictions and failings that I needed expert help to face.

I found that expert help in a Jungian analyst, Dr. Nathan Schwartz-Salant. In Nathan I found a humble adept of the process of embodiment, someone whose writing and work was inspired by a commitment to an ancient alchemical vision of the transmutation of the whole being through the integration of the shadow. I knew on meeting Nathan that I could speak of anything with him; nothing human or divine is foreign to him. And I knew he was the right person with whom to take my journey into the shadow, because he conveyed to me some of the solid dignity of my own father, and because that force of presence was accompanied by great learning, a fierce but respectful heart, rich mystical understanding, and a shamanic gift for interpreting dreams.

With Nathan I uncovered within myself the "five inner saboteurs" I have already described, and began to uncover the ways they hooked into my own childhood traumas and relationships and distorted the evolution of my path. This was grueling and, at first, shaming, but because I was accompanying this descent with mystical meditation and sacred body work, I found myself strong enough to integrate what I was discovering. My recommendation to you is that you undertake deep shadow work only with the help of an expert and in conjunction with sacred meditation and body practices.

Through this process, I discovered that coming to accept the secret link between my shadow and the shadow that drives every corrupt politician, every dangerous pervert, every tyrant, every exploitative CEO, began to erode the self-righteousness and secret sense of superiority, even elitism, that had always been my deepest spiritual enemies. In coming to accept the reality of my own collusion with everything I feared and hated, I achieved a richer self-knowledge and a clearer, less sentimental, more skillful understanding of others and of the workings of power in the world.

In this process of descent, I was also brought to confront different levels of resistance in my body, both feeling the stored-up grievances of the past in it and allowing the Light to descend into it to work and penetrate. Until you face your loathing for and terror of the body, you can never understand why the human race has launched a war on Nature it is doomed to lose. You have to confront all the inherited religious messages about the body's illusion or evil, all your own fears and dislikes about your own body and the depth of your fear of death. This work of facing the darkness in your own psyche and uncovering the levels of stored suffering, self-disgust, cultural conditioning, and innate resistance in your body slowly starts to shatter the narcissism of your false self, constructed over a lifetime, and opens you to the grace of the Divine and the liberating power and joy of your own Divine Self.

The Sacred Activist will have to encounter two highly evolved forms of narcissism in himself—the narcissism of the mystic and the narcissism of the activist. One of the reasons why the mystical renaissance is not as powerful as it should be and activists are not as persuasive and skillful as they need to become is because both groups, though made up of intelligent and concerned beings, suffer from their own forms of narcissism that only shadow work can expose, transform, and heal.

The mystic's shadow of narcissism manifests as an addiction to transcendence, as an escapism from responsibility from the real, as a sometimes passive and childish belief that the Divine will take care of everything, and as a subtle but devastating denial of the reality of evil and the heartbreaking misery of the world. In the course of my path I have succumbed to all of these forms of narcissism; I see now how resourcefully I justified and even celebrated them with the same ingenuity that a drug addict uses to justify his addiction.

The activist's shadow of narcissism is many-sided, subtle, and lethal; I have seen it, too, in myself. This narcissism manifests, I have found, as a messiah complex, as a dark ego-reinforcing delight in humiliating and destroying one's opponents, and as a depreciation of ordinary life in favor of heroic sacrifice. It also manifests as an addiction to doing for its own sake, with exhaustion, body neglect, and burnout seen as signs of authenticity and badges of courage.

If the Sacred Activist does not address both of these narcissistic shadows in herself and face them squarely and without illusion, they will continue to have unconscious power over her and block the Birth of the Divine Human. No one should imagine that the process of facing the shadow is anything less than devastating. As the Prophet Muhammad said, drawing on his own experience, "If

The Law of Constant, Humble Shadow Work

I described openly the enemy in your lives, even the heart of the brave would be shattered."

But this shattering of the "heart of the brave," as the prophet knew, is essential to make the brave both wiser and more authentically strong. Without being shattered in this way, you cannot begin the work of uncovering and releasing the positive forces of passion and instinctual power that are hidden in your shadow and that you need for your sacred work in the world. The elements of shadow that are dangerous, even demonic, when unacknowledged can—when made conscious and worked on perseveringly in Divine Grace—become sources of lucid strength, instinctual self-protection, and patient energy, as well as of a forgiving but shrewd compassion for all other beings who are caught in the same fierce struggle.

I have come to discover that in working with both the shadow of the mystic and the shadow of the activist, great and transforming help comes from what I call the "essential divine nature" of both. I have described Sacred Activism as the "third fire" created by the fusion of the fire of the mystic's sacred passion for God and the fire of the activist's sacred passion for justice. If you accompany your descent into the shadows of the seeker and activist with a commitment to fuse their two sacred fires, you discover a marvelous alchemical secret: the shadow of the mystic's addiction to transcendence can be illumined and transformed by the sacred fire of the activist's passion for justice, whereas the shadow of the activist's addiction to immanence, to radical action for its own sake born out of sacred outrage but unillumined by sacred wisdom, can be illumined and transformed by the mystic's sacred fire of joy and surrender to divine guidance.

By fusing the two sacred fires of the mystic's passion for God and the activist's passion for justice into the third fire, you start to feel far more unified with reality. You find yourself entering more and more, through no will of your own, into union with the One in the core of ordinary life—shopping, eating with friends, typing at your desk, or walking in the park. By undertaking the work of marrying your light and dark opposites within yourself, you are led by the synchronistic magic of the Eternal Alchemy into a deeper union with the One, grounded in life, whose consummation constitutes true freedom.

I do not want you to imagine that I live in this experience of freedom all the time. You cannot live in it all the time because, as my doctor Nathan once said, "every moment you have to die into it to be able to live in it." The freedom bestowed by the marriage of the light and dark within you is not an experience you can control. If you try to control this Divine Freedom, it dissolves and vanishes. You have to surrender, and go on and on surrendering, mind and heart, soul and body, to the One, dying into its eternal life each moment, in constant paradoxical embrace of a death that is simultaneously a birth.

As this paradoxical embrace becomes more and more natural to you, you connect, more and more and in expanding wonder, with the Force of Divine Love that starts to illumine your mind, inflame your heart, and vibrate in the cells of your body. This entry into the One's unified field is the Birth; the birth is engendered by the Light out of the Darkness.

The descent into the shadow is inescapable and essential to the authentic Birth. It is one of the holiest of mysteries, the place where the greatest treasures are to be found. When you discover the diamond hidden at the heart of this paradox, it irradiates your whole being with an ever-expanding joy, wisdom, and hope.

CHAPTER 14

THE LAW OF JOY

The sign that you are beginning to enter into communion with the One is that you experience the beginnings of what I call the Great Joy, with its triumphant Yes that dances through, within, and above all the One's terrible and amazing games of opposites. This Great Joy is known by all authentic mystics as the ultimate reality of God and, therefore, of all realities created from that ultimate reality.

Sacred Activism at its highest and deepest is this Joy, this Yes, in action. What the process of Radical Embodiment I have described births in you—in your mind, heart, and body—*is* this Great Joy. With the ecstatic and lucid hope that arises from such an experience, and with the power of Divine Grace that flows effortlessly through such joy, you can endure any ordeal, transmute any difficulty, and surmount any obstacle. The power of this Great Joy is the power of Sacred Activism. Sacred Activists' most holy and beautiful responsibility to themselves and to others is to live as much as possible in this joy with its generosity of tenderness toward all beings and all things.

The purest sacred transmission of this joy as the secret of reality and the source of sacred action is given to us, I believe, by the Taittirya Upanishad. These words that come from the highest truth proclaim the richest, most whole, and most hopeful vision for human life I know. I am quoting the Upanishad at length because I want to invite you to savor the interconnected majesty and unity of this vision. Please read slowly, bringing your whole self and everything I have tried to convey in this book to this unfolding of ancient, but timeless, wisdom:

Bhrigu went to his father, Varuna,
And asked respectfully: "What is Brahman?"

Varuna replied: "First learn about food,
Breath, eye, ear, speech, and mind; then seek to know
That from which these are born, by which they live,
For which they search, and to which they return.
That is Brahman."

Bhrigu meditated and found that food
Is Brahman. From food are born all creatures,
By food they grow, and to food they return.
Not fully satisfied with his knowledge,
Bhrigu went to his father, Varuna,
And appealed: "Please teach me more of Brahman."

"Seek it through meditation," replied Varuna,
"For meditation is Brahman."

Bhrigu meditated and found that life
Is Brahman. From life are born all creatures,
By life they grow, and to life they return.
Not fully satisfied with his knowledge,
Bhrigu went to his father, Varuna,
And appealed: "Please teach me more of Brahman."

"Seek it through meditation," replied Varuna,
"For meditation is Brahman."

The Law of Joy

Bhrigu meditated and found that mind
Is Brahman. From mind are born all creatures,
By mind they grow, and to mind they return.
Not fully satisfied with his knowledge,
Bhrigu went to his father, Varuna,
And appealed: "Please teach me more of Brahman."

"Seek it through meditation," replied Varuna,
"For meditation is Brahman."

Bhrigu meditated and found that wisdom
Is Brahman. From wisdom come all creatures,
By wisdom they grow, to wisdom return.
Not fully satisfied with his knowledge,
Bhrigu went to his father, Varuna,
And appealed: "Please teach me more of Brahman."

"Seek it through meditation," replied Varuna,
"For meditation is Brahman."

Bhrigu meditated and found that joy
Is Brahman. From joy are born all creatures,
By joy they grow, and to joy they return.

Bhrigu, Varuna's son, realized this Self
In the very depths of meditation.
Those who realize the Self within the heart
Stand firm, grow rich, gather a family
Around them, and receive the love of all.

Respect food: the body is made of food;
Food and body exist to serve the Self.
Those who realize the Self within the heart
Stand firm, grow rich, gather a family
Around them, and receive the love of all.

Waste not food, waste not water, waste not fire;
Fire and water exist to serve the Self.
Those who realize the Self within the heart
Stand firm, grow rich, gather a family
Around them, and receive the love of all.

Increase food. The earth can yield much more.
Earth and space exist to serve the Self.
Those who realize the Self within the heart
Stand firm, grow rich, gather a family
Around them, and receive the love of all.

Refuse not food to those who are hungry.
When you feed the hungry, you serve the Lord,
From whom is born every living creature.
Those who realize the Self within the heart
Stand firm, grow rich, gather a family
Around them, and receive the love of all.

Realizing this makes our words pleasing,
Our breathing deep, our arms ready to serve
The Lord in all around, our feet ready
To go to the help of everyone in need.
Realizing this we see the Lord of Love
In beast and bird, in starlight and in joy,
In sex energy and in the grateful rain,
In everything the universe contains.

Drawing on the Lord's resources within,
Security, wisdom, and love in action,
We conquer every enemy within
To be united with the Lord of Love.

The Self in man and in the sun are one.
Those who understand this see through the world
And go beyond the various sheaths

The Law of Joy

Of being to realize the unity of life.
Those who realize that all life is one
Are at home everywhere and see themselves
In all beings. They sing in wonder:
"I am the food of life, I am, I am;
I eat the food of life, I eat, I eat.
I link food and water, I link, I link.
I am the first-born in the universe;
Older than the gods, I am immortal.
Who shares food with the hungry protects me;
Who shares not with them is consumed by me.
I am this world and I consume this world.
They who understand this understand life."

The Taittirya Upanishad is giving us a vision of divinized life, a divinized life lived naturally in the the world and in the family, expressing itself naturally in loving service and action. In this vision, all of reality is known as sacred; physical desire is known as holy and its passion-energies as divine; the joy of Divine Love embodied in the human flows out as a cherishing of all sentient beings. All of life becomes the sacred theater of an unfolding revelation of unity with all things and beings in the One, and this unity expresses itself naturally in joyful sacred service.

The Birth that is taking place on the earth, with Sacred Activism as a midwife, is a birth of this holy, integrated, and profoundly joyful vision. Just to experience this vision as a reality, as I am beginning to, is to have the highest, deepest, most potent kind of hope. If this Great Joy is born in me, in its fragmentary beginnings, how could it not be the secret potential of every other human being? Since this Great Joy is known and felt as divine, what possible limits to its transforming power could there be? What difficulties, however terrible, could it not transfigure? The secret of the Taittirya is the secret of reality, of "beast and bird," of "starlight," of "sex energy," of "grateful rain," of "everything the universe contains."

Evolutionary mysticism adds another dimension to the Taittirya Upanishad's vision of this joy worked out in reality: it recognizes the Great Joy as the power behind evolution itself. It recognizes that this Great Joy is the power of Divine Love that, in its passion for self-discovery and self-giving, has created a universe that it is constantly evolving in and from itself, transforming and resurrecting it in every moment out of an ecstasy of creativity. This vision of the evolutionary power and ecstatic creativity of the Great Joy is the gift of the Divine Feminine, who draws us at once ever upward and ever downward, to birth in us the union of opposites through which a wholly new power of transforming action flows in a river of Divine Grace.

To live this all-unifying and transforming joy in the core of life, and to act from its passionate compassion and with the power of its grace, is the wonderful and hopeful task of the Sacred Activist. What the return of the Divine Feminine gives us, with its revelation of joy as the resurrecting power of the universe, is sacred permission to know all our many joys in life as having their origin in the Great Joy. When we know this, we can experience each of them as different facets of the Diamond of the One, turned to us ceaselessly to illumine, strengthen, encourage, and unify us. As Rumi writes:

Whatever inspires the mind is of the perfume of my
    Beloved,
Whatever fires the heart is a ray from my Friend.

In practice, for me, this means trying to live seven kinds of sacred joy, separately and together, at the core of my life. They are for me the seven facets of the Diamond of the Great Joy.

THE JOY OF INSPIRATION

As the process of Embodiment has deepened in me, so has my gratitude for the inspiration I find in the great sacred texts of all traditions, in mystical poetry, and in all the arts, especially music. In Rumi's poetry I hear the voice of God; in Bach's music I hear the intricate harmonies of the Dance of Opposites in the One. Without mystical, artistic, cultural inspiration, it is hard to remain infused with purposeful joy, and I urge all activists to find in the beauty of the arts a reflection of that Beauty that creates the universe and so is the ultimate source of all truly sacred action.

THE JOY OF BEING IN NATURE

In these last years, my love of every aspect of Nature has become both more intense and more tender. When I am inwardly turned to the Beloved, all of Nature is revealed as radiant with the Presence; every stone and flea and squirrel and human being and the whole of Nature appears as a ceaselessly flowing epiphany of the Radiance. "Adore and love Him," Rumi writes, "and He will reveal to you that everything is a drop from His river of infinite splendor."

THE JOY OF SACRED FRIENDSHIP

If it takes a village to raise a child, it takes several villages of wise, tender, compassionate experts to midwife a Birth. As I go farther on my own Path, the holiness of my deepest friendships and the joy they initiate me into becomes ever more vivid to me. The work I have begun to do on my own shadow has enriched my knowledge and love of my friends and deepened my compassion for them, which only increases my admiration for the resources and dignity they bring to their own struggles.

Coming to experience and celebrate the holiness of sacred friendship and to be grateful for the wisdom of your friends increases your faith in life and your capacity for skillful action. Coming to savor the tenderness of the Friend expressing itself through all the many kinds of friendship in life brings you, by degrees, into the secret unity of life in the Mercy of the One.

I used to make the mistake of thinking that friendship had to take second place to my work. Now I realize that was part of both my mystic and my activist shadow, and I understand that the joy friendship brings me is the clue to doing my work as an act of friendship toward all beings. As I experience the Joy of the Friendship of the One through all the many joys of human friendship, my innate friendliness toward all beings becomes more confident and generous and suffuses the work I do with its warm light.

THE JOY OF SACRED FRIENDSHIP WITH ANIMALS

Purrball, the cat that I lived with for two years during my marriage, changed my life. Her love for me and my love for her came with the force of a revelation. I had never imagined that an animal could be capable of such heights of devotion or that I would find in my heart such depths of abandoned tenderness for a small tortoiseshell tabby, wobbly on her legs. It was a holy love on both sides, and it opened me to the possibilities that the Birth of the Divine Human offers us for a wholly new level of communion with animals. This communion is essential to their and our survival; it is also the source of a wonder and a joy in creation that makes you long to do everything you can to protect life in all its forms.

All animal lovers know this joy and know it as one of the wonders of life. In the name of this joy, and with this joy, we must all now call out to the human race to stop its barbaric treatment of animals, not only because it is wrong in itself, but also because it prevents us from communing with them as sacred relations and from learning their lessons of love and loyalty, harmony with nature, and serenity before life and death. The hope in our best selves that streams to us from the eyes of every respected and well-treated animal is a hope we cannot afford to do without.

THE JOY OF SACRED TANTRA

My marriage initiated me into the ecstasy and generosity of Tantric sexuality, of a sexuality that is consciously consecrated to

Divine Love and is thus graced with the bliss-energies of the eternal lovemaking of the Father-Mother in the One. To be illumined, sustained, and increasingly permeated by this ecstasy and generosity, you need to, of course, do constant shadow work on your own drives to possess, manipulate, and control; on your body shame and your guilt about sexual pleasure; and on your own subtle desires to appropriate the power such an experience gives you for your own purposes and not those of the Divine.

But if you do this shadow work humbly, and in the contest of rigorous spiritural practice and if you are blessed to find someone you can love with sacred passion who is also committed to doing his or her shadow work and spiritual practice, then you can experience in the core of your life the great and transforming blessing of Tantric love and the bliss-energies of faith and hope and persistence that it floods you with.

As this revelation deepens in you, what you come to discover is that Tantric sexual ecstasy with another person opens you up to experiencing the same ecstasy, in a subtler, softer form, in your relations with all of reality. A sacred eros is awoken in you that opens its arms in love to all things and all beings and hold them to your heart. When all your actions are suffused by this "secret" sacred eros, they become ripe with blessing.

THE JOY OF LOVING THE HOLY
WITH HEART AND MIND AND BODY

This joy is for me the holiest and most empowering of all the joys we can experience with another human being. I am not talking here about a guru-disciple love, although I know from my own adoration of my ex-guru and the graces it gave me that even in a hierarchical or unequal setting, to experience another being as holy and to love that being with *your* whole being can be transformative.

The relationship I am describing here is the one I have known with three different men and with one woman whom I never met, but whose films and photographs have amazed and inspired me. The men I have introduced to you in the book—Thuksey Rinpoche, the Dalai Lama, and Father Bede Griffiths. The woman is the great Indian teacher, Sri Anandamayi Ma, whose sacred beauty in all her stages of life poignantly reflects the beauty of the Mother's passion and compassion. I turn in my heart to all of these beings, and I love them with my whole mind and heart and body. As I do so, a subtle transmutation of my whole being takes place: a kind of radiant contagion spreads from them to me, a contagion of joyful embodied presence.

While no human being is free of faults or shadow, some human beings embody the beauty, passion, and compassion of the Divine more transparently than others. Loving these transparent beings with devotion and gratitude, naturally, without needing to idealize them but recognizing and revering them as holy, starts to make *you* more transparent and illumine your being with grace.

The guru system has tried to corral this powerful holy love for its own hierarchical and exploitative uses. The truest expression of this holy love, however—as Jesus and other realized sages showed us, and as Father Bede Griffiths showed me—is in a relationship of intimacy and equality, qualities that for me characterize the authentically holy (along with a sense of humor). In loving such beings whose intimacy with and humility toward you humbles you in turn, you start to become more intimate and humble with others and to radiate increasingly toward them, in your ordinary life, the same sacred transparence.

THE JOY OF PLAY

The two mystical images of God that are the most inspiring and revelatory for me are the Golden Dancer and the Divine Child. They open up in me the dimension of sacred love and sacred action as play, which is an essential attribute of joy.

The Golden Dancer is Shiva, the Dancer worshipped throughout South India, most particularly in the temple of Chidambaram in South India. When I first saw there the golden image of the Dancer God, I was elated. I recognized it as a sign from the Divine to us of what *we* as human beings could become if we, through the grace of the dancer's alchemy, learned to dance with joy in all the opposites of life. Shiva, the Divine Dancer, dances exotically and serenely in each of the opposites—in destruction as well as creation, death as well as birth, agony and defeat as well as rapture and victory: in learning to dance as God dances, in all the opposites with serenity and joy, our human dross is turned into divine gold, and our lives and the actions flowing form them become a golden dance, radiant with divine mystery and grace.

The Divine Child, the Sacred Androgyne, is an image for God found in almost all the esoteric mystical systems. This Divine Child is engendered by an inner marriage of the Sacred Masculine and the Divine Feminine, of mind and heart, soul and body, vision and action. The Child is in secret, humble, and wonder-struck union with the One, and expresses the joy of this union.

I constantly meditate on and try to integrate myself with these two interdependent images of the Divine, because as I do so, what is revealed to me and in me is that sacred action is best undertaken as a form of sacred play. To call it play does not mean that the work of Sacred Activism is not grave and serious in many ways, or not concerned with life-and-death issues. Yet if sacred action is dominated by too great a seriousness, it can easily veer into self-righteousness and self-admiration and become offensive to others. If our sacred action is informed too much by a view of our situation as tragic and urgent, it will not be balanced by the transforming peace and delight of the Divine Bliss and it cannot be sustained by the secret joy of God, which could otherwise see us through even the worst ordeal.

Here, again, we reach a marriage of opposites that the images of Golden Dancer and Divine Child are slowly initiating me into. It is this marriage of opposites—of gravity with play; of humor with passion; of concern for the humility, accuracy, and focus of our work with unconcern for its immediate results—that slowly begins to free you to move into the dimension of the One, for whom even the terrible and amazing adventure of evolving the Divine Human through our current crisis is a form of free, wild, holy play. What wilder, freer game, after all, could the Divine play than birthing itself in us to change us into itself?

BIRTHING THE DIVINE CHILD IN THE MOTHER

Let me now offer a practice I love that will help you experience your whole being as a temple of the Great Joy, from which all sacred action flows in a mystery of sacred play to bless, heal, and restore.

This practice—which I have adapted from an ancient Hindu Tantric practice—introduces anyone who performs it with focused devotion to the ecstatic wholeness of being and the integration of heart, mind, body, and soul that the Mother aspect of God is trying to birth in all of us.

The holy Indian woman who taught me this practice 20 years ago in Benares told me: "Always begin it by as deep a meditation as you can manage on what it would be like to live as a fully empowered Divine Child of the Father-Mother. Imagine with the full powers of your sacred imagination exactly what it might be like to live a life in which heart, mind, body, and soul were all experienced as different facets of one Divine Joy. Try to imagine what a great healing of all fears and false division such an experience would bring you and how, finally, it would illumine every thought and emotion and action. Try to imagine what an energy of ecstatic creativity such a living knowledge of joy would flood your whole life with.

"Then," she added, "when you have inspired yourself with a vision of the fully active, passionate, creative, healed, and balanced Divine Child you long with every cell of your entire being to become, invoke as fervently as you can the direct aid of the Mother aspect of God, the Divine Mother, in all Her glory of light power, to come and transform you. This is important; for the practice to be as powerful as it can be, you must begin it by this fervent, passionate, and wholehearted invocation of the light power of the Divine Mother. If you call on Her with the force of your whole being, She cannot refuse to come to you immediately, and you will feel a new strength and sense of purpose start to flood not only your mind and spirit but also your body."

Begin the practice, then, by imagining the wonderful new powers and energies that becoming the Divine Child will bring you, and by invoking with passion the light power of the Divine Mother.

After this period of intense and focused meditation, start the following visualization with faith that it can and will act as an instrument of the birthing power of the Divine Mother. Know that it can and will, if you do it regularly, birth more and more completely in you the Divine Child you essentially are, and liberate you from all concepts, inherited prejudices, and psychological and physical imbalances that prevent you from attaining effortless trust.

Imagine now the Divine Mother, in whatever form you worship her most readily, standing in the shining air above your head with Her palms outspread. Imagine whatever form of Her you have chosen—Kali or Durga or the Virgin of Guadalupe—surrounded by blazing golden light and smiling with joy and compassion. Imagine now that from Her outspread palms She starts to pour a living, glittering stream of soft golden light above your head. Know that this golden light has within it every power of Divine Joy, every power of gnosis, healing, and integration. Know this with your whole being and surrender to its operation in calm and perfect trust.

At this stage, I find that it sometimes helps me to say inwardly again and again, "O light of the Mother's great joy, heal me and transform me, illumine my mind and open my heart! Heal my body of its fears of separation! Integrate completely my heart with my mind, my body with my soul, and bring me whole and joyful into the blaze of your Presence!" The more devotedly I can invoke the healing and transforming powers of the light, the more powerfully I feel its operation.

Now allow the stream of living golden light from the outspread palm of the Divine Mother to enter your body through the spiritual center that is in the crown of your head. It is this center, the Hindus and Buddhists believe, that connects us to the Transcendent.

Let the golden light of the Great Joy now pour into and fill your head. As it does so, pray particularly for your powers of vision and understanding of the sacred to be awakened and strengthened. At this stage, many people will find that they feel a kind of tickling or pressure between the eyebrows; this is the light starting to awaken what Eastern mystical tradition calls the ajna chakra, or Third Eye. The Third Eye, the spiritual eye, is located in the center of the forehead and is opened slowly through prayer, meditation, and service. When it is completely open, the Third Eye sees Divine Light dancing in reality and knows the whole universe as the living dance of light consciousness.

Now invite the light reverently down into your throat. In the Eastern mystical systems, the spiritual center in the throat controls communication of every kind. Allow the golden light to open that center now as strong sunlight opens a shy red rose. Imagine the red rose of effortless communication, truth, and love opening in your throat, slowly but certainly, as the divine sunlight of the Mother's light is trained on it.

Your head and your throat are gently on fire. Take that golden fire of the Great Joy down into your shoulders and along your arms to the very tips of your fingers, imagining as you do so that every cell in that part of your body awakens to its essential divine strength and life.

Now take the golden light of the Mother down into your heart center, about an inch to the right of the middle of your chest. The fully awakened heart is the core and guide of your Divine Human being; awakening to its boundless love and all-embracing sky-like clarity is the most crucial aspect of the Birth you are allowing the Mother to prepare in you. So as you take the golden light of the Mother's Great Joy down into your heart, pray to the Mother to open your heart completely and to reveal the whole universe

The Law of Joy

blazing in its subtle fire, and to keep your heart open in Her forever. As you do so, start to feel how your light-opened heart, through Her grace, aligns head and emotion, mind and psyche, your physical and your spiritual being. Pray for this supreme sacred balance of heart and mind, soul and body, heaven and "earth," inner and outer, masculine and feminine, to become ever deeper and ever richer in you and to inspire in you ever more profound realizations of the truth of unity.

By opening your vision, communication, and heart centers through the grace of the Mother's golden light, you have now begun the birth of the Divine Child in you and established yourself in the living presence of Divine Love. Relish this ecstatic and blissful Presence and call out to it inwardly with words of welcoming adoration. Knowing the Child is being consciously born in you, thank and adore the birthing Mother with all the ecstasy of your awakening sacred heart.

Now, with faith, trust, and confidence, take the golden light down into the rest of your body, marrying it and all of its conscious and unconscious movements, hungers, passions, and desires with the love power of the light. To make this wedding of the rest of the body with the awakened heart-light as rich and complete as possible, it is best to perform it in stages.

First, take the golden light down into your belly, allowing it to become pregnant with the light's full strength and sweetness. In the belly there is a spiritual center that ensures balance in the deepest sense by grounding illumination in the real. As you take the golden light into the belly, pray for it to mature and deepen this grounding power so that you can incarnate in all your emotions, acts, and thoughts more and more of the Mother's love and force.

Confident that you are established in sacred balance and in Divine Love, fearlessly lower the full force of the Mother's light into your genital area. So much of human ignorance and violence and suffering come from sexual wounding and from the millennia of shame and body hatred imposed on us by most of the world's religions. The Mother, however, wants all of our instincts to be consecrated to God, and She is preparing for Her children a way to a sanctified sexuality, a direct way of delighting in the divine energies that engender and sustain the creation and a direct initiation into the mysteries of divine human love. So, as you lower golden light into your genital area, pray to the Mother to remove all your guilt and shame, all the fears inside you that prevent you from acknowledging and consecrating the intrinsic holiness of your sexual nature. Ask the Mother to transform your sexual nature into an instrument of divine human love, not by repressing your physical desires but by divinizing them.

One very powerful way of imagining this divinization of sexuality is to picture your genitals before the light enters them as a dull grayish-black crystal. As the light of the Great Joy floods them, imagine this grayish-black crystal starting to blaze with golden brilliance. Sustain the meditation until you can visualize the whole genital area as one soft, radiant blaze of crystalline golden light.

Now continue taking the light of the Great Joy even further down—down your thighs, through your kneecaps, down the backs of your legs, and down through your ankles to the ends of your toes. In many of the Eastern mystical systems, the spiritual centers that govern the life of the unconscious are hidden in the lower part of your body. Pray to the Mother to clarify, purify, and divinize all the secret movements of your subconscious to help you make all its darkness conscious and to open up all the traumas, humiliations, and fears that are hidden there to the light of divine healing.

Every part of you—body, heart, mind, and soul—is now alight with the golden fire-light of the Divine Mother's supreme joy. Relish the power of electric balance that streams in and from you. Let your entire body-soul-breath-mind blaze in praise of the Mother who has birthed you into your wholly healed, transformed, Divine Human being.

Now, in the final moment of the practice, slowly take the golden light back up through every center, one by one, blessing each one with the light's healing power again. As the light enters each center from the bottom upward, slowly, one after the other, pray that all remaining obscurities and blocks in your Divine Human nature be removed forever.

Let the light travel back into your head and then sit on top of your crown center like a large, pulsing fireball. Balance it there for one long, calm moment, Then, concentrating your entire being in one huge inward shout of ecstatic joy, drop the fireball above your crown center deep into your sacred heart and let it explode there like a bomb of light, sending brilliant golden light in vast pulsing waves of healing bliss in all directions.

Imagine as your heart explodes that it is a birthing supernova of Divine Fire and that radiation from its birth is now expanding and extending throughout the universe.

Rest calmly and humbly in this power that has now been born in you through the Mother's grace and your cooperation with it. Pray that all beings may be filled with this power and inspired by it to preserve and transform our world.

CHAPTER 15

THE LAW OF
NETWORKS
OF GRACE

In a recent article in *The New York Review of Books,* Bill McKibben wrote: "The technology we need most badly is the technology of community—the knowledge about how to cooperate to get things done. Our sense of community is in disrepair."

It is essential, therefore, that Sacred Activists, while pursuing their individual spiritual paths and embracing their own specific kinds of service, learn to work together and to form empowering and encouraging "networks of grace"—like-minded, like-hearted beings brought together by passion, skill, and serendipity in order to pool their energies, triumphs, grievances, hopes, and resources of all kinds. When people of like mind and heart gather together, miraculously powerful synergy can result.

Such networks of grace can only be as transformative as our crisis requires if those who form them work constantly to resist the seductions of power, glamor, and celebrity and develop ever-deeper discrimination. Learning to distinguish the real gold—authentic networks of grace—from the false glitter of networks of power and self-importance is difficult; it demands prayer, humility, patience, shadow work, and the unglamorous ability to wait on results, not force them before the Mystery has had a chance to form them completely.

THE GROUNDING OF THE VISION

Now I want to offer my plan—a plan that is already taking shape—for helping to ground and embody this vision as practically and effectively as possible.

About three months ago, I went to teach a course in Sacred Activism in a convent in Cleveland, Ohio. I had been praying for a long time to understand how best to organize Sacred Activism, and the night before, a vision of what is possible had come to me in a dream.

I was lying in bed reflecting on the success of Al Qaeda and certain fundamentalist Christian groups. Fanaticism, it seems, can always organize itself brilliantly; it is ordinary, good, concerned people who find it hard to mobilize their efforts. This has to change, and change fast, for the Birth to be effective.

From my study of terrorist and fundamentalist organizations I had learned one essential thing: that the success of their movements relies on "cells," small self-contained groups of between 6 and 12 people who encourage, sustain, and inspire each other with sacred reading and meditation and share each other's victories and defeats in the course of what they believe is sacred action. Such an organization of interlinked small cells is the key to the horrible effectiveness of Al-Qaeda and the reach of the major fundamentalist ministries.

The word *cell* immediately made me think of a revealing conversation I had had with Deepak Chopra the year before. Deepak spoke to me at length of how the process of transformation in and through the Dark Night that we are now enduring could be compared to the different stages of a caterpillar's transformation into a butterfly. He described how the caterpillar spins a cocoon around itself and dissolves inside the cocoon into a featureless gray gunk. This gray gunk Deepak compared to the chaos and confusion of the Dark Night, a chaos and confusion that is also pregnant with new possibilities—pregnant, in fact, as he said, with the birth of the butterfly, "the new Divine Human," which is a being as genetically and physically different from the caterpillar "as a bicycle is from a Lear jet."

It was the way Deepak described this birthing process that struck me. He described how, when the gray gunk has liquefied to a certain point, cells he called "imaginal cells" are genetically awoken in it. These cells feed off the gunk for their growth as they increasingly cluster together, creating, through a synergistic alchemy, the body and wings of the future butterfly.

As I lay on my bed in the convent in Ohio, the connection— between my vision of the interlinked cells that could organize Sacred Activism and Deepak's description of the imaginal cells that could create the butterfly of the Divine Human—became diamond-clear. I understood that my networks of grace were to be a network of imaginal cells, individual cells of 6 to 12 people praying and meditating together, inspiring each other, and acting together for local or international causes of their own choosing.

The next day, I spoke of my embryonic vision to the nuns of the convent and to the 70 people assembled for the workshop. The first cell of Networks of Grace was established later that day. Since then, whenever I have spoken of this plan, it has aroused a delighted response; as of this writing, there are a dozen Networks of Grace cells around the country.

It is my prayer that this book and the vision of Sacred Activism it embodies will inspire the spread of interlinked cells of Networks of Grace all over North America and the world. The time has come, in Teilhard de Chardin's words, to harness the energies of love, and so for the second time in the history of humanity discover fire—in this case a grassroots movement of the sacred fire of Sacred Activism organized through Networks of Grace.

As I continued to pray and meditate on this vision of the imaginal cells of Networks of Grace, I began to study how President Obama had conducted his campaign largely by mobilizing grassroots forces. One of the main secrets of his success was an

innovative Internet campaign that connected millions of his sup-
porters and gave them hope and inspiration for change. Organizing the imaginal cells of Networks of Grace, or, rather, inviting
people to organize themselves in their local communities and connect with other cells in other communities through the Internet,
became the obvious next step in growing the vision. I now knew
why I had bought the domain name NetworksofGrace.org two
years earlier.

I have, as you can see, a big and global vision for Networks
of Grace—but the truth is that such things best start small, on a
local level. So let me propose to you reading this book now that
when you have finished it and had time to think about it clearly,
you ring up between 6 and 12 of your friends and start a Network
of Grace in your local community devoted to Sacred Activism. I
do not in any way want to control the evolution of Networks of
Grace, but if my vision of Sacred Activism has inspired you to your
own vision of change you want to implement with the help of
others, I would be honored and delighted.

Let me suggest three ways you might organize these cells:
around profession (with lawyers, politicians, doctors, therapists,
and so on, all wanting to devote their common skills to a common
cause), around passion (for animals, art, meditation, or healing,
for example), or, as I suggested in Chapter 8 when I outlined the
five forms of service, around heartbreak (such as cruelty against
animals or environmental degradation). Any of these three foci
could provide an admirable way of gathering like-minded hearts
around you and pooling your resources and creativity to start
inspiring and sustaining each other in action.

Imagine cells of concerned lawyers working together to see
that people trapped in foreclosure get proper legal representation.
Imagine cells of doctors pledging to work together give free treatment to the millions in this country and all over the world who
cannot afford health care. Imagine cells of therapists pledging to
offer Sacred Activists free shadow work. Imagine what cells of concerned politicians could do with common creativity and passion,
from passing imaginative energy and environmental legislation to

addressing such causes as gay marriage, and animal rights. Imagine what cells of parents and professionals could achieve to help those going through financial crisis: collecting food and clothing, taking children to school, helping people out of work find jobs. The very extent of our growing crisis makes the applications of the vision of Networks of Grace almost infinite.

I would like to ask four things of these cells and their members to keep them aligned with the spirit of Sacred Activism. First, that each session begin with at least a quarter of an hour of meditation, prayer, or the reading of sacred texts. Second, that everyone in the cell commit to consistent spiritual practice. Third, that, as far as possible, the meetings of the Network of Grace be conducted in an atmosphere of joy, possibly with food and drink to deepen fellowship. Fourth and finally, that, after people have gotten to know one other, some sort of sober, intimate, and kind shadow work be conducted among the members to help keep the Network of Grace from being manipulated by the egos of the members or by the sometimes destructive dynamics that can dominate group discussion and behavior. The best way I have found of working with such destructive dynamics is to note them immediately when they occur and then break the group into pairs to work on, firstly, what has been revealed individually and collectively, and secondly on what needs to be remedied. Sharing the sometimes luminous (and sometimes hilarious) wisdom that arises in such honest discussion can lead to surprising transformation. If this foundation of spiritual practice, joy, fellowship, celebration, and humble shadow work is laid down from the beginning, the work that is achieved through a Network of Grace will be inspired, grounded in, and blessed by the One.

THE GLOBAL
CURRICULUM FOR
SACRED ACTIVISM

For those who want to study in greater depth the vision of
Sacred Activism, evolutionary mysticism, and the Path of Radical
Embodiment, I have founded the Institute for Sacred Activism in
my hometown, Oak Park, Illinois, which has a long history of supporting liberal and spiritually progressive causes. Starting in April
2009, I embarked on a journey with 40 other Sacred Activists from
all walks of life to create a Global Curriculum for Sacred Activism
based on four initiations designed to bring together the world's
spiritual and practical wisdom to illumine our crisis.

We plan to finish the Global Curriculum in its initial form by
the end of 2009. I envision the curriculum changing and expanding
as the crisis changes and as new realizations of the Birth and new
forms of wisdom about it are given to us. This curriculum will be
distributed in print, on DVD and cassette, and via the Internet in
languages from Chinese to Hindi and Swahili, along with the vision
of Networks of Grace, for anyone who wants to work with them.

Ever since the vision of Sacred Activism started to take shape
in me, my deepest concern has been how to *ground* it How to
keep it from being an inspiring abstraction and bring it to life in
practical terms. In these two projects—the Networks of Grace and
the journey with others to create a Global Curriculum for Sacred
Activism—I pray that this essential grounding of the vision of the
Birth in the practical is off to a helpful start. I welcome any of your
suggestions and ideas, and I would be honored if you wrote to me
at andrew@instituteforsacredactivism.org.

Starting in 2010, I will be teaching the Global Curriculum in
a series of four initiations for Sacred Activists at my institute in

Oak Park. I intend to keep tuition to a minimum, and I hope to get funding for scholarships so people with more enthusiasm than money can attend. Please join us. Dates will be posted on my Website: **www.andrewharvey.net**.

AFTERWORD

In our time we have come to the supreme adventure of our evolution, in which we will, by channeling the energies of love in Sacred Activism in response to a perfect storm of crises, transform both life on earth and ourselves. May all who come to this book know the great peace and hope that flow from knowing this adventure to be blessed by the Divine. May all who come to this book and embrace the truth of Sacred Activism understand in heart, mind, soul, and body and remember always what Mother Teresa is telling us when she writes:

> We all long for heaven where God is, but we have it in our power to be in heaven with Him right now—to be happy with him at this very moment. But being happy with Him now means:
>
> > Loving like He loves,
> > Helping like He helps,
> > Giving as He gives,
> > Serving as He serves,
> > Rescuing as He rescues,
> > Being with Him 24 hours a day—
> > Touching Him in his distressing disguise.

Let us always remember what another great Teresa, the sixteenth century Spanish saint Teresa of Ávila, would have us understand (in words I have adapted to embrace the mystical truth of all religions):

> The Divine has no body now on earth but yours,
> No hands but yours,

No feet but yours,
Yours are the eyes through which to look out
The Divine's compassion to the world;
Yours are the feet with which
The Divine is to go about doing good;
Yours are the Hands with which
The Divine is to bless all beings now.

In accepting the tremendous and glorious challenge of these words, we become transformed; in enacting their truth with courage we transform our endangered world, through the all-powerful grace, and with the blessing, of the Divine that longs to birth itself in every aspect of our inner and outer lives.

ACKNOWLEDGMENTS

To all those, such as Jim Hollis, Andrew Beath, Joan Chittister, Julia Butterfly Hill, Seane Corn, Matthew Fox, and Michael Lerner, who are pioneers of spirit-based activism. Thank you for your magnificent work that continues to inspire me with hope.

To Patricia Gift, dear friend and wise, loving editor.

To Laura Koch, for her patience and professionalism.

To Anne Barthel, for her matchless polishing.

To my agent and friend, Ned Leavitt, for his faith and encouragement.

To Kitty Farmer, for her help and belief during a dark time.

To Cathy Towle, for all her kindness, imagination, and work. I shall always be grateful for the joy we shared.

To Carol Mason, for her loyalty, perseverance, and fun, and for her immaculate typing.

To Jill Mangino, for her beautiful soul.

To Lekha Singh, for suggesting the word *sacred* in sacred activism and for her brilliance and generosisty.

To Dolores Myss, for her unfailing love.

To David Smith, for his friendship and wisdom.

To Mona Lisa Schulz, for her wildness, brilliance, and wit.

To Susan Rosen, for her passion and for the support of Miriam's Well, Saugerties. Thank you for offering me the perfect laboratory for working out the vision of this book.

To Jim Garrison, for his championing of Sacred Activism at Wisdom University and his example of stamina and dedication.

To Toni Cook, for her fire and for the support of Saint Paul's Church, Denver.

To Carolyn Rivers, for her wisdom and the support of The Sophia Institute, Charleston.

To Marj Britt, for her tender friendship and the support of Unity Church Tustin.

To Barbara Booth, for her courage and for the support of the Sacred Wisdom Center of Guelph, Ontario, Canada.

To Felicia Tomasko, for her tireless work and faith and for the support of LA Yoga.

To Louise Palmer, for her brilliance, sensitivity, and advocacy.

To Joan Oliver, for the delight of our long friendship.

To Ludwig Max Fisher and Gabriella Martinelli, for their love and faith.

To Bhikku Bodhi, for the example of his selfless service and for his clear advice.

Grateful acknowledgment is made for permission to reprint excerpts from the following works: Selections from the Chandogya and Taittirya Upanishads reprinted by permission from the Upanishads, translated by Eknath Easwaran, founder of the Blue Mountain Center of Meditation, copyright 1987, 2007; reprinted by permission of Nilgiri Press, P.O. Box 256, Tomales, CA 94971, www.easwaran.org; selections from *Blessed Unrest* by Paul Hawken (New York: Viking Penguin, 2007); selection from *The Mother* by Sri Aurobindo (Pondicherry, South India: Aurobindo Ashram Trust); selections from the I Ching, or Book of Changes, translated by Richard Wilhelm (Princeton: Princeton University Press, 1967). All Rumi translations are by Andrew Harvey and are adapted from previous versions for this book.

GLOSSARY

The Black Madonna. A dark image of the Virgin Mary worshipped initially in medieval France and Italy and then all over the Catholic world. Her darkness relates her to Eastern images of the Divine Feminine, such as Kali, and to Isis, the Egyptian Divine Mother. Marion Woodman describes her force in *Dancing in the Flames:* "She is blunt, neither indulgent nor sentimental. She demands embodiment. Living in the creative intercourse between chaos and order, she calls us to enter into the dance of creation."

Bodhicitta. *Bodhi* is Sanskrit for "our enlightened essence," and *citta* translates as "heart," so *bodhicitta* is the desire to attain perfect enlightenment to be of the greatest help to sentient beings.

Bodhisattva. A realized being who renounces liberation or Nirvana to remain in cyclical existence to help until all sentient beings are saved.

Brahman. Sanskrit for the non-dual absolute Reality without properties, the Ground of Being.

chakra. Sanskrit for one of the seven centers of psychic energy in the body.

chthonic. Of or relating to the earth or "underground world," from the Greek *Chthon* earth.

Divine Consciousness. Blissful, direct, non-dual awareness of the One appearing in and as all things.

Divine Feminine. The feminine side of the Divine, which expresses itself as mercy and unconditional compassion and both creates the universe and lives in it in every aspect, detail, and process.

Divine Human. The next evolutionary stage in human development a realized and increasingly divinized human being working humbly with the One to transform life on earth.

Embodied Godhead. Another term for the Divine Feminine or Mother; the creation or universe as manifestation of the Divine Light in which the Light lives in and as every thing.

evolutionary mysticism. Mystical systems that seek the union of the whole being—heart, mind, soul, *and* body—with the One in order to birth spirit in the deepest recesses of matter and so engender a new kind of human being, the Divine Human (see above). Such mystical systems include that of Jesus in the Gospel of Thomas, certain strains of esoteric Christianity, the various alchemical systems, some versions of the Kabbalah, and certain schools of Hinduism and Mahayana Buddhism. In the 20th century, five great evolutionary mystics gave us their visions of how the transfiguration of the human into the Divine Human would take place: Sri Aurobindo, the Mother (Sri Aurobindo's mystic partner), Satprem, Teilhard de Chardin, and Father Bede Griffiths.

fana. Islamic mystical term for the annihilation or dissolution of the ego or nafs (false self) that leads to *baqa,* or constant normal indwelling in Divine Consciousness.

Force of Divine Love. The power of all-transforming grace inherent in and emanating from the Divine Love that creates all things and worlds.

Glossary

Grail. A cup or plate that according to medieval legend was used by Jesus at the Last Supper and later became the object of many chivalrous quests. It is the ultimate quest object in esoteric Christianity.

hexagram. A figure of six lines or sides (from the Greek *hex,* "six"). The Chinese divination classic the I Ching consists of 64 hexagrams with attendant commentaries. Each of the hexagrams (*qua* in Chinese) represents one stage of the interconnected processes of cyclic change.

Ishq. Arabic for love, ardent devotion, intense passionate adoration. As a divine attribute, Love, for the Islamic mystic, is the force that drives the universe and brings about both the Creation and its return to Oneness.

karma. The universal law of causation of actions.

Karma Yoga. The way of selfless service, of service dedicated wholly to the Divine.

Kali. Hindu representation of God as both creative and destructive Mother, usually represented as black and garlanded with heads.

Mantra. A sacred syllable, word, or phrase of spiritual significance or power.

Path of Radical Embodiment. The Way of evolutionary mysticism that leads to the birth of the Divine Light in the cells of the body, the increasing divinization of the whole human being, and the enactment of Divine Love and Divine Wisdom in sacred action.

Shakti. The divine creative energy personified as a feminine principle; the spouse of Shiva.

Shiva. One representation of the supreme Godhead, in Hinduism: God as creator and destroyer, usually represented in male form as a dancer.

Sufism. The Islamic path to direct realization of the unity of God through love, knowledge, and surrender.

Tantra. A set of rigorous disciplines in Hinduism and Buddhism. These interlinked mental, spiritual, physical, and sexual disciplines enable the devoted and skilled practitioner to experience directly the inter-relation of the One and the many, Reality and "appearance," absolute and relative.

theosis. A term in the mystical theology of the Greek Orthodox Church for the Divine transfiguration of the human being through prayer, ecstasy, and surrender (from Greek "theos" – God).

transcendent. Being above and independent of the material universe; said of the Divine.

Upanishad. The wellspring of India's spiritual philosophies. Said to be about three thousand years old, these texts are the earliest living record of what Aldous Huxley called the "Perennial Philosophy"—the certainty, born out of direct personal experience, that there is a spark of divinity in every being, and that to realize union with the Self is the goal of human life. Etymologically, the word *Upanishad* in Sanskrit suggests "sitting down near," that is, at the feet of an illumined adept in an intimate setting.

RECOMMENDED READING

FIVE BOOKS ON EVOLUTIONARY MYSTICISM

1. Sri Aurobindo. *The Life Divine* (India; Sri Aurobindo Ashram; 1977)

2. Bede Griffiths, ed. Bruno Barnhart. *The One Light*: Bede Griffith's Principal Writings (Templegate Publisher, Springfield, Illinois: 2001)

3. The Mother. *The Agenda*, Volumes 1–13. (Mira Aditi Press, Mysore)

4. Satprem. *The Adventure of Consciousness.* (Institut de Recherches Evolutives, Canada)

5. Teilhard de Chardin, trans. Bernard Wall. *The Divine Milieu.* (New York: Harper and Row, 1960)

FIVE BOOKS ON THE DIVINE FEMININE

1. Sri Aurobindo. *The Mother* (India; Sri Aurobindo Ashram 1972)

2. Anne Baring and Jules Cashford. *The Myth of the Goddess: Evolution of an Image* (New York: Viking Press. 1991)

3. Andrew Harvey. *The Return of the Mother* (Tarcher Putnam, 2001)

4. Miranda Shaw. *Passionate Enlightenment: Women in Tantric Buddhism.* (Princeton, New Jersey: Princeton University Press, 1994)

5. Marion Woodman and Elinor Dickson. *Dancing in the Flames: The Dark Goddess in the Transformation of Consciousness* (Boston: Shambhala, 1997)

SIX BOOKS ON THE CONTEMPORARY
CRISIS AND SPIRIT-BASED ACTIVISM

1. Andrew Beath. *Consciousness in Action: The Power of Beauty, Love and Courage in a Violent Time* (Lantern Books, 2005)

2. Paul Hawken. *Blessed Unrest: How the Largest Movement in the World Came into Being and Why No One Saw It Coming* (Viking, 2007)

3. David C. Korten. *The Great Turning: From Empire to Earth Community* (Kumarian-Berrett-Koehler, 2006)

4. Paul Roga Loeb. *Soul of a Citizen: Living with Conviction in a Cynical Time* (St. Martin's Press, 1999)

5. Michael Lerner. *The Left Hand of God: Taking Back our Country from the Religious Right* (Harper San Francisco, 2006)

6. Elaine Prevallet. *Towards a Spirituality for Global Justice: A Call to Justice* (Sowers Books, 2005)

ABOUT THE AUTHOR

Andrew Harvey is an internationally acclaimed poet, novelist, translator, mystical scholar, and spiritual teacher. He was born in South India in 1952, moved to England at age nine, and later attended Oxford University, where in 1973 he became a Fellow of All Souls College. In 1977, he returned to India for the first time since his childhood and underwent several mystical experiences, which began a series of initiations into different mystical traditions to learn their secrets and practices.

Harvey has taught at Oxford University, Cornell University, Hobart and William Smith Colleges, The California Institute of Integral Studies, and the University of Creation Spirituality (now Wisdom University), as well as at various churches and spiritual centers throughout the United States, England, and Europe. He is the author of more than 25 books, including *Son of Man, The Direct Path, Hidden Journey, The Essential Mystics, The Way of Passion: A Celebration of Rumi, The Return of the Mother, A Journey in Ladakh,* and his most recent work, *Sun at Midnight: A Memoir of the Dark Night.*

Harvey was the subject of the 1993 BBC documentary *The Making of a Modern Mystic* and has appeared in several others, including *Rumi Turning Ecstatic, The Return of Rumi, The Consciousness of the Christ,* and a documentary on the life and work of Marion Woodman. His own 90-minute documentary *Sacred Activism* was produced by the Hartley Film Foundation in 2005. Several of his lectures are available on **www.myss.com** and on YouTube (see Website below for contact information).

He is the founder and director of the Institute for Sacred Activism in Oak Park, Illinois, where he lives. His Website is: **www.andrewharvey.net**. He can be contacted at: **andrew@instituteforsacredactivism.org**. He is available for interviews, lectures, courses, workshops, and one-on-one spiritual direction.

NOTES

NOTES

NOTES

NOTES

NOTES

NOTES

Hay House Titles of Related Interest

YOU CAN HEAL YOUR LIFE, the movie,
starring Louise L. Hay & Friends
(available as a 1-DVD program and an expanded 2-DVD set)
Watch the trailer at: **www.LouiseHayMovie.com**

THE SHIFT, the movie,
starring Dr. Wayne W. Dyer
(available as a 1-DVD program and an expanded 2-DVD set)
Watch the trailer at: www.DyerMovie.com

*THE BIOLOGY OF BELIEF: Unleashing the Power of
Consciousness, Matter & Miracles,* by Bruce H. Lipton, Ph.D.

*CHANGE YOUR THOUGHTS—CHANGE YOUR LIFE:
Living the Wisdom of the Tao,* by Dr. Wayne W. Dyer

FRACTAL TIME: The Secret of 2012 and a New World Age,
by Gregg Braden

*THE FUTURE IS NOW: Timely Advice for
Creating a Better World,* by His Holiness the Karmapa

*POWER, FREEDOM, AND GRACE: Living from the
Source of Lasting Happiness,* by Deepak Chopra

*SPONTANEOUS EVOLUTION: Our Positive Future (and a Way to
Get There from Here),* by Bruce H. Lipton, Ph.D., and Steve Bhaerman

WRITING IN THE SAND: Jesus & the Soul of the Gospels,
by Thomas Moore

YOUR SOUL'S COMPASS: What Is Spiritual Guidance?
by Joan Borysenko, Ph.D.

All of the above are available at your local bookstore,
or may be ordered by contacting Hay House (see last page).

We hope you enjoyed this Hay House book.
If you'd like to receive our online catalog featuring
additional information on Hay House books and products,
or if you'd like to find out more about the
Hay Foundation, please contact:

Hay House, Inc.
P.O. Box 5100
Carlsbad, CA 92018-5100

(760) 431-7695 or (800) 654-5126
(760) 431-6948 (fax) or (800) 650-5115 (fax)
www.hayhouse.com® • www.hayfoundation.org

Published and distributed in Australia by: Hay House Australia Pty. Ltd.,
18/36 Ralph St., Alexandria NSW 2015 • *Phone:* 612-9669-4299
Fax: 612-9669-4144 • www.hayhouse.com.au

Published and distributed in the United Kingdom by: Hay House UK, Ltd.,
292B Kensal Rd., London W10 5BE • *Phone:* 44-20-8962-1230
Fax: 44-20-8962-1239 • www.hayhouse.co.uk

Published and distributed in the Republic of South Africa by: Hay House SA
(Pty), Ltd., P.O. Box 990, Witkoppen 2068 • *Phone/Fax:* 27-11-467-8904
info@hayhouse.co.za • www.hayhouse.co.za

Published in India by: Hay House Publishers India, Muskaan Complex,
Plot No. 3, B-2, Vasant Kunj, New Delhi 110 070 • *Phone:* 91-11-4176-1620
Fax: 91-11-4176-1630 • www.hayhouse.co.in

Distributed in Canada by: Raincoast, 9050 Shaughnessy St., Vancouver, B.C.
V6P 6E5 • *Phone:* (604) 323-7100 • *Fax:* (604) 323-2600 • www.raincoast.com

Take Your Soul on a Vacation

Visit **www.HealYourLife.com**® to regroup,
recharge, and reconnect with your own magnificence.
Featuring blogs, mind-body-spirit news, and life-changing
wisdom from Louise Hay and friends.

Visit **www.HealYourLife.com** today!

HEAL YOUR LIFE ♥

Take Your Soul on a Vacation

Get your daily dose of inspiration today at **www.HealYourLife.com**®. Brimming with all of the necessary elements to ease your mind and educate your soul, this Website will become the foundation from which you'll start each day. This essential site delivers the latest in mind, body, and spirit news and real-time content from your favorite Hay House authors.

Make It Your Home Page Today!

www.HealYourLife.com®

HAY HOUSE